STRANGE BUT TRUE
GEORGIA

STRANGE BUT TRUE GEORGIA

LYNNE L. HALL

SWEET
WATER
PRESS

TABLE OF CONTENTS

In A Strange State:

Road Trip Through Strange But True Georgia

Got Georgia on your mind? The Georgia Department of
Industry, Trade, and Tourism sure hopes so. Visit their state and
they promise to show you rolling rivers, charming towns, and
bustling cities. Read their brochures, watch their slick
commercials, and you'll be regaled by the Peach State's many
scenic beauties. And, no doubt about it, there are plenty to see.
Jawjah is the quintessential Southern state, rich in history, and
marked by the sharp contrasts of its past and present. You can
stroll down peaceful wisteria-draped lanes with magnificent
antebellum homes. That is, after you've barreled your way
through the hubbub of Hartsfield International Airport and
navigated the confusing tangle of streets and avenues of
Hotlanta!

At the state's northern end, you'll find breathtaking
mountain vistas. The Appalachian Trail begins here, in Fannin
County, "Gateway to the Blue Ridge Mountains." Southward
there are vast areas of quaint rural countryside, filled with those
charming small towns. Verdant hillside settings bump against
Tennessee and Alabama to the west, and to the east you'll find
the deep blue waters of the Atlantic seashore. That's the
tourism department's Georgia—elegant, stately, beautiful.

Ahh, but we've got a different Georgia in mind. Beneath all
that elegance, stateliness, and beauty lies a whole other state,

and it's a state of pure wackiness, a state filled with quirky characters, extraordinary happenin's, weird and spooky places, and some of the most bizarre landmarks ever built. Forget about those purple mountain majesties and wisteria-scented lanes. We've got goofy giant peanuts and the Pig Hill of Fame! There are giant rabbits and chickens, a big ol' Co-cola, and a slew of weirded-out museums.

So drop that colorful tourism brochure. Turn off the pretty commercials. Come tour the Strange But True Georgia on our minds!

Strange Statues

Scattered willy-nilly across Strange But True Georgia is an eclectic collection of strange and quirky monuments. You'll find a whole crew of Muffler Men, some really big fruits and nuts, giant animals, including the world's largest metal elephant, and the weirdest Statue of Liberty you'll ever hope to see.

It's A Zoo Out There!

The Georgia countryside is covered with all kinds of animals!

ABSTRACT IRON HORSE • WATKINSVILLE

In 1954, a civic-minded sculptor donated an abstract iron statue of a horse to the University of Georgia. The statue was placed in an open courtyard where, for reasons unknown, students took an instant dislike to it and tried to burn it. They must've been pretty drunk, because, remember, the horse is made of iron.

Anyway, the university was in a quandary about

The Iron Horse once stood in a courtyard on the University of Georgia campus. It was removed after students tried to burn the sculpture.
Courtesy of UGA Alumni Association

what to do with the horse, until a Watkinsville farmer offered to take it off their hands. He placed it in his cornfield, where it stands today.

Located on Highway 15 South, two miles outside Watkinsville.

BIG CHICKEN •
MARIETTA

Marietta has a Big Chicken. This 56-foot steel wonder was erected in 1963 as an advertising gimmick for Johnny Reb's Chick, Chuck and Shake, the local greasy spoon. Designed by an Atlantic Steel engineer, the chicken's eyes rotated and the beak opened and closed. A ruffle on its head waved in the Southern breeze.

The Big Chicken has been a Marietta icon since 1963.
Photo by Zeny Williams

For decades, the Big Chicken served as a landmark for locals. Directions were always given in reference to the chicken, as in "Take a left just past the Big Chicken." Time marched on, the jaunty ruffle fell to disrepair, and then suffered severe storm damage in January of 1993. It looked as if the Big Chicken was doomed to that giant fryer in the sky.

But, wait! It's KFC to the rescue. When the venerable Kentucky Fried Chicken bought the restaurant, Big Chicken and all, their first idea was to raze the chicken and rebuild in their own image. Public outcry put an end to that idea, and good ol' KFC magnanimously restored the chicken to its former glory—rotating eyes, flapping beak, and all. There's even a gift shop located inside the chicken that sells all manner of Big Chicken memorabilia. And, best of all, Marietta citizens still have their point of reference…. "Go two miles south. If you pass the Big Chicken, you've gone too far."

Located at the junction of U.S. 41 and State Highway 120.

BIG COW • SAVANNAH

Savannah's Big Cow stands outside Keller's Flea Market. She's fifteen feet tall, twenty-two feet long, and weighs 1500 pounds!

Located at 5901 Ogeechee Road.

BIG RABBIT • RABBITTOWN

Geez! It's the Easter bunny on steroids!

Big Cow stands proudly outside Keller's Flea Market.
Courtesy of Keller's Flea Market

Actually, the 20-foot rabbit greeting you outside the

The Big Rabbit greets visitors outside the Rabbittown Café.
Photo by Zeny Williams

Rabbittown Café is this town's tribute to those wascally wabbits what gave their lives to save Depression-era citizens from certain starvation. Back during the lean times of the Great Depression, and many years before the ubiquitous yard bird became the dinner of choice, this north section of Gainesville was known for its rabbit industry.

Fortunately, the South soon discovered fried chicken, and little bunnies everywhere were spared. Today, at the Rabbittown Café you can find all manner of delicacies, except one. You'll find no wabbits on the menu.

Located at 2415 Old Cornelia Highway.

BRER RABBIT • EATONTON

Eatonton's statue of Brer Rabbit, commissioned in 1955 by the Women's Club, is quite a bit smaller than Rabbittown's big bunny, but it's no less historic. Eatonton was the home of Brer Rabbit's creator, Joel Chandler Harris, author of *The Tales of Uncle Remus.* In keeping with Brer Rabbit's dapper personality, the cast iron statue sports a red smoking jacket, white dress shirt, and blue necktie. Ever the gentleman, he's holding a long-stemmed pipe. His contemplative expression hints at some tomfoolery in the offing. For many years, he graced the lawn of the Putnam County Courthouse, but was recently moved to the Uncle Remus Museum.

Located at 214 Oak Street.

Brer Rabbit stands in author Joel Chandler Harris's hometown of Eatonton.
Photo by Becky Jones

CAPITOLINE WOLF • ROME

"Well, I'll swan, Mabel. Would you look at that!" You might have overheard that comment had you attended the 1929 unveiling of the statue of the Capitoline Wolf. Heck, you might've even been the one making the comment!

The statue depicts the mythical story of twins Romulus and Remus, sons of Mars, the god of war and Rhea Silvia, daughter of King Numitor of Alba Longa. When King Numitor was overthrown by his evil brother, Amulius, the twins were ordered to be cast into the Tiber River. A kindly slave placed the babies into a reed basket (hmmm…shades of Moses) and set it loose on the river, where they were rescued by a she-wolf. The wolf nurtured the twins until they were found and raised by a local shepherd.

When the twins were grown, they reclaimed Alba Longa for King Numitor and decided to build a city nearby. In an argument over the name of the city, Romulus killed Remus, which meant, by golly, he could name the city just any old thing he wanted to. And that's how Rome (that Eye-talian one) got its name.

The Capitoline Wolf depicts mythical twins Romulus and Remus, who were nurtured by a she-wolf.
Photo by Zeny Williams

The statue, an exact replica of the one that stands in the Palazzo dei Conservastori on Capitoline Hill in Rome, Italy, was an official gift to Rome, Georgia, from the governor of Rome, Italy. It was commissioned by Dictator Benito Mussolini himself, when the Chatillion Corporation Silk Mill of Milan relocated to this fair city in 1929.

The statue's unveiling was a bit of shock to Southern sensibilities. Though many appreciated it as a work of art, many were offended by it and felt it was not something that should be viewed by ladies and children. Often, when events were scheduled at the City Auditorium, where the statue was displayed, the twins were diapered and the wolf was draped. In 1933, some wag absconded with Romulus—or was it Remus?—a crime that was never solved. Through the efforts of the Rotary Club, however, a replacement twin was sent from Italy.

When the Italians declared war on the Allies in 1940, the statue was in grave danger of being dynamited by local patriots. It was removed to storage for safe keeping, where it languished for twelve years. In 1952, through the efforts of citizens and art lovers, the Capitoline Wolf, with those hungry twins, was returned to the pedestal in front of City Hall, where it now holds a place of honor.

Located at 601 Broad Street.

KADIE THE COW • COLUMBUS

Kadie the Cow has been a Columbus fixture for more than fifty years. She began her career as the mascot of local Kinnett Dairy, where she stood outside the main entrance until the dairy closed a few years ago. After a brief retirement, she returned to the

Kadie the Cow and little BeBe proudly guard their home outside Best Buy.
Courtesy of Roadsidenut.com

parking lot of the local Best Buy store—and there's good news! Kadie now has a young'un! Local residents awoke one morning in 2003 to find a mysterious calf next to Kadie. No one even knew she was expecting!

Rustlers briefly absconded with the fiberglass calf, named BeBe in a recent naming contest, but authorities located her months later in a dumpster outside of town. Best Buy cleaned her up and cemented her next to Kadie, where she stands today.

Located at 2995 Manchester Expressway.

PIG HILL OF FAME • ELLIJAY

"Look, Pa, Them's Pigs!" Them are Pigs. And they're all over the hillside! The Pig Hill Of Fame got its start as an advertising gimmick for Poole's Bar-B-Q. When owner and entrepreneur extraordinaire Colonel Oscar Poole was denied the right by the state to place a sign on the highway, he came up with the idea to place plywood pigs on the hillside behind his campy restaurant. He started with ten pigs, all with names of family members painted on them. The idea caught on, and soon, Poole was giving customers the opportunity to have their names immortalized on one of his plywood pigs. Today, more than three thousand pigs crowd the hill, with more being added each day.

Eat at the restaurant—which is touted by critics as some of the state's best bar-b-cue—and you, too, can be added to the Pig Hill of Fame. Just three things are required: an honest face, good intentions, and, oh yeah, $5. Got to defray those plywood and paint costs somehow.

Located at 164 Craig Street.

Rosie the Elephant • Ringgold

Rosie, "The World's Largest Metal Elephant," graces the rose garden of Windwood Garden Center. Rosie is sixteen feet tall, twenty-four feet long, and weighs six tons. Her creator, Larry Holcomb, owner of the garden center, applied to the *Guinness Book of World Records*, only to be told that a man in India was building a larger elephant. Since there's no projected completion date for the Indian elephant, however, Rosie can lay claim to the World's Largest title for the time being.

Located at 5342 Battlefield Parkway.

The Storyteller • Atlanta

OK. We don't know if this qualifies as an animal statue or not. We do know that Atlanta's Buckhead section, in the heart of the Bible Belt, is a strange place to find a pagan sculpture, but, hey, there it is! The bronze sculpture is of a storyteller. Seated on a log, with lanterned staff in hand, he's holding court to an assortment of bronze woodland creatures. The weird thing is that he has

The Storyteller holds court to an assortment of bronze woodland creatures.
Photo by Zeny Williams

the body of a man (naked!), with an antlered buck head (yeah, yeah, we get it).

The Storyteller, also called The Buck Man, is the creation of Alabama artist Frank Fleming, who created an eerily similar sculpture titled The Ram Man for Birmingham, Alabama's Five Points South section. Fleming says his half-human, half-animal sculptures are not a product of paganism, but rather a result of his rural upbringing, where he learned of the kinship between animal and human behavior.

Located at the corner of Peachtree and Roswell Road in the Buckhead section of Atlanta.

Muffler Men and Waving Women

THE DRAGONSLAYER • MARIETTA

The Dragonslayer, a massive three-ton chrome tableau of a knight battling a dragon, depicts the myth of St. George, the patron saint of England. Supposedly, the story is an allegory representing Christianity overpowering paganism.

According to the myth, a huge and frightful dragon lived near a tiny village in a land far, far away. The dragon demanded a portion of every hunt from the villagers, but one day, all the animals had been slain, and so the villagers had nothing to offer the dragon. Fearing his wrath, they sent the beautiful young daughter of a villager as an offering.

As the fearsome dragon approached the young maiden, already tasting bar-b-cue, no doubt, George the knight stepped in and killed the beast, saving the maiden. Returning her to her village, George told the overjoyed villagers of Jesus Christ and baptized them all.

Marietta's Dragonslayer was created by sculptor Sean Guerrero for Aspen Productions, an events production company. Both knight and

St. George, The Dragonslayer, stands poised, ready to defend goodness and right.
Photo by Zeny Williams

dragon are fashioned entirely of recycled items, including the chrome remains of 1930s-era automobiles. St. George, armor glinting in the Georgia sun, braces the massive dragon with sword upraised, poised to strike a blow for goodness and right.

Located at 1685 Terrill Mill Road SE.

DUTCHY • ELBERTON

Elberton bills itself as the Granite Capital of the World, and truly, it does manufacture a lot—more granite monuments than any other city in the world. Their first monument, however, had quite an ignominious beginning. The monument honoring the Confederacy, the first produced by Elberton's first granite finishing plant, was commissioned by the ladies of the town's Confederate Memorial Association. The order was simple: A statue of a soldier dressed in a Confederate Army uniform. What could go wrong?

Strange Statues

The statue's unveiling on July 15, 1898, was planned with much fanfare. An immense crowd gathered and as the band struck up a tune, the statue was unveiled, but instead of the expected cheers, there was stunned silence. The statue was kinda squatty-looking—ugly, really. There was a bewildered look on his face, and many locals thought the bushy mustache made him look like a Dutchman. And, Lord, what's that he's wearing? That Confederate monument looked to be wearing a Yankee uniform!

Dutchy was the first monument created by Elberton's granite finishing plant.
Courtesy of the Elberton Granite Association

Disgruntled townspeople dubbed the seven-foot statue Dutchy. Over time, their distaste for him grew, until finally they lynched him. On the morning of August 14, 1900, the town awoke to find Dutchy toppled from his finely-wrought, 22-foot pedestal, where he lay in a broken heap. He was buried there at the foot of the pedestal.

But that's not the end of the story. In 1982, the Elberton Granite Association, Inc., the company that produced Dutchy, located the statue's burial site and carefully exhumed him. Restored to his former glory and now fondly referred to as Old Dutchy, he occupies a place of honor in Elberton's Granite Museum and Exhibit.

Located on Highway 72 at One Granite Plaza.

The world's largest largemouth bass was caught in Telfair County. On June 2, 1932, fisherman George Perry pulled the 22-pound, 4-ounce behemoth from Montgomery Lake off the Ocmulgee River.

THE FLAIR • ATLANTA

Here's a guy in a right peculiar position. The Flair is a bronze statue that was sculptor R. MacDonald's gift to Atlanta to commemorate the 1996 Olympic Games held there.

The twenty-six-foot statue depicts a male gymnast performing a flair, a strength move where the athlete, with all his weight on his hands, swings his legs into the air. Performing the move atop an Olympic ring, the statue has an intense look on his face and muscles popping out everywhere. His left leg almost touches his left ear and the right leg is extended. At the base is a brass plaque stating:

"The great tradition of Western art has been and should continue to be, not merely representational work but the idealization of the human form, the glorification of both heroic individuals and the heroic possibilities of mankind." Pierce Rice

Strange Statues

Located in the Georgia World Congress Center at Andrew Young International Boulevard NE in downtown Atlanta.

MUFFLER MEN • ALBANY/ ATLANTA/ DOUGLAS/ VALDOSTA/ WASHINGTON

Georgians seem to have an affinity for Muffler Men. There's a smattering of the big hunks scattered across the state.

A Paul Bunyan Muffler Man stands in front of the Albany Auto Repair. A patriotic sort, he's holding an American flag. Located at 2421 Stuart Avenue. There's a handsome Muffler Man at 3495 Norman Berry Drive in Atlanta. In Douglas, a Muffler Man wearing a sea captain's hat stands guard along U.S. Highway 441.

Hey, this guy is a real Muffler Man! That is, he's a large statue made from a bunch of old mufflers. He stands in front of, what else? A muffler shop. Recycling at its best. Located one mile east of I-75—across from the Wal-Mart—in Valdosta.

Washington's Muffler Man, which stands in front of Jones Brake & Muffler, must be good luck. In January 2005, owner James Jones won $130 million in the Georgia lottery. Maybe Jones will share the riches and get MM some fancy duds to wear—maybe replace that tire in his hand with a gold-handled cane or something.

Located on Robert Toombs Avenue.

STATUE OF LIBERTY • MCRAE

Carried away by a fit of patriotism following the country's centennial celebration, the Lions Club of McRae in Telfair

County decided that a replica of the Statue of Liberty was in order. Unfortunately, their funds didn't match their zeal. There was no money to hire a sculptor and no cash for materials. Undaunted, they decided to make it a do-it-yourself project, using materials (read "junk") they could pick up around town.

They pulled a stump from a nearby swamp, and using photographs of the real Miss Liberty, they fashioned the head with a chainsaw. Her arm is made from Styrofoam, and the hand holding the torch is an electrician lineman's glove. A coat of green paint, and voilà! Lady Liberty, Southern-style!

Their enthusiasm unquenched, the Lions Club then took down the town's old fire bell and put a crack in it. Miss Liberty was mounted on a pedestal with the homemade Liberty Bell nearby, and on July 3, 1986, the town's Liberty Square was officially dedicated.

The town of McRae is proud of its Miss Liberty. Short on funds, the Lions Club used materials found around town to build her.
Courtesy of Telfair County Chamber of Commerce

Miss Liberty stands there today in all her trashy glory. She's thirty-five feet tall and is a 1/12th scale version of the original

Strange Statues

Statue of Liberty. Though many would proclaim her to be less than pleasing in the looks department—OK, many would say she's ugly—the town and Telfair County are exceedingly proud of her and the Southern ingenuity that went into her creation.

Located at the intersection of Highways 341, 23, 441, 319, and 280.

STONE MOUNTAIN RIDERS • STONE MOUNTAIN

Georgia's Stone Mountain is the largest known exposed granite formation in the world. Rising 1,683 feet above sea level, it was formed when magma forced its way out of the Earth's molten center 350 million years ago. Millions of years of erosion eventually exposed the granite's sparkling surface and pocked it with large indentions that during the spring and summer months fill with water. You'd think, because of their temporary existence, these "vernal (spring) pools" might be pretty to look at, but devoid of life. You'd be wrong. Two species of microscopic shrimp—fairy

Stone Mountain is the world's largest known exposed granite formation. The mountain features Confederate heroes Davis, Lee, and Jackson.
Courtesy of Stone Mountain Park

and clam—live out their lives in the pools, laying their eggs in the granite crevices. Though the adult shrimp die when the pools dry up in late summer, the eggs survive, and when spring once again brings the rain, the eggs hatch and the cycle continues.

The world's largest exposed granite should have the world's largest high-relief sculpture, don't you think? The Stone Mountain Confederate Memorial carving depicts Confederate heroes President Jefferson Davis, General Robert E. Lee, and General Thomas "Stonewall" Jackson astride their fiery steeds. Towering 400 feet above the ground, it measures 90 feet by 190 feet and is recessed 42 feet into the mountain. It's so large that a person can easily stand inside the shelter of a horse's nostril, as did many a workman when hit by an unexpected rainstorm. The deepest point is at Lee's elbow, which measures twelve feet to the surface.

The carving was the idea of Helen Plane, a charter member of the United Daughters of the Confederacy (UDC). It took four years of negotiation, but in 1916, the UDC convinced the mountain's owners to deed them the mountain's north face. The UDC was given twelve years to complete a Civil War monument.

It took a little longer.

In 1916, sculptor Gutzon Borglum was appointed to carve the memorial by the Stone Mountain Monumental Association. Because of that pesky World War I and funding problems, the project was not started until 1923. Using dynamite, Borglum blasted away huge portions of the mountain and completed Lee's head on January 9, 1924. A good start, we guess, but, oops, in

Strange Statues

1925, a dispute arose with the association. Miffed to the max, Borglum picked up all his models and sketches and left the state—for South Dakota, where he actually completed a mountain sculpture. You may have heard of it—Mount Rushmore?

Anyway, work resumed on Stone Mountain in 1925, when sculptor Augustus Lukeman signed on for the job. The three central figures of the Confederacy were his idea. He removed Borglum's work and using pneumatic drills, worked diligently on the project. By 1928, a new version of Lee's head was completed, but, unfortunately, the original twelve-year deadline was up and funds were depleted. The owners reclaimed the property, and for thirty-six years, Lee's head remained alone and lonely there on the mountain face.

Then in 1958, the state purchased the mountain and surrounding land. Another association was formed—comprised of six internationally-known figures in the art world. A competition was held, with nine world-renowned sculptors submitting designs for a new sculpture. In 1963, the Stone Mountain Memorial Association chose sculptor Walker Kirkland Hancock of Gloucester, Massachusetts (What? A damn Yankee?) to finally complete the project.

Work began in 1964, and Lee once again lost his head, but he got it back soon enough. With a new technique using thermo-jet torches, workmen were able to remove tons of granite daily. The torches also allowed the detail of a fine painting, carving eyebrows, strands of flying mane, buckles, and capes.

The Confederate Memorial Carving was finally dedicated on May 9, 1970. Today, Stone Mountain Park, a theme park, operates on the land surrounding Stone Mountain. It includes lodging, rides, exhibits, a museum, and best of all, a sky lift up the mountain, where you can see the ghost riders and their steeds up close and personal.

Located 16 miles East of Atlanta on Highway 78.

THE WAVING GIRL • SAVANNAH

The Waving Girl statue stands on the eastern end of Savannah's River Street. It's a statue of a girl, waving a large cloth at something in the distance. A dog sits placidly at her feet.

Waving Girl Florence Martus greeted some 50,000 ships while living at the Elba lighthouse.
Courtesy of www.savannah-visit.com

The waving girl is Florence Martus, who was born and raised on the nearby coastal island of Elba, where her father was the lighthouse keeper. It was the late 1800s, and there wasn't a lot for a girl to do on such a small island. Perhaps to pass the time, Florence took to waving a white handkerchief at passing sailors as their ships sailed in and out of Savannah. At night, she would wave a lantern. Sailors would notice and send greetings of their own.

On one fateful evening, Florence became more than just a

girl waving a handkerchief—she became a hero. When a nearby river dredge caught fire, Florence and her brother rowed out in their skiff to rescue thirty drowning sailors.

Many speculated that Florence's hanky-waving vigil was spurred by love for a young sailor who had promised to someday return for her, but who sailed away, never to be seen again. Whatever the reason, Florence continued her vigil for forty years, greeting each ship as it sailed passed. Many a lonely sailor penned letters to her, addressing them simply to "The Waving Girl."

Fruits, Nuts, and Coca-Colas
BIG COCA-COLA • ATLANTA

Got yourself a powerful thirst? Well, hie on down to Atlanta's Turner Field where you'll find a really big, really strange bottle of Co-Cola (that's Coca-Cola to all you Yankees). OK, so maybe you won't be able to quench your thirst with this particular bottle, but it's definitely worth a looksee.

Perched high above left field, this eclectic folk-art bottle is comprised completely of everyday items you'd find on a baseball field. It contains:
- 60 shoes
- 2000 coke cans
- 48 batting helmets
- 18 catcher's mitts
- 86 fielder's gloves
- 290 bats
- 6680 baseballs

- 24 jerseys
- 64 bases
- 16 chest protectors
- 24 pitching rubbers (not gonna ask!)

Oh, yeah, and while you're there, you might wanna catch the Braves game!

Turner Field is located at 755 Hank Aaron Drive in Atlanta.

Georgia was named for King George II of England.

BIG RED APPLE • CORNELIA

Georgia is known for its peanuts, peaches, and pecans. So why does Cornelia have a Big Red Apple? Well, there's a story behind that.

It was the 1920s. The Great War (WWI) was over and cotton was king of the South. The agricultural extension agents, aware that a cotton crop failure would wipe out the majority of Southern farmers, sought to introduce diversification. In some counties, they introduced dairy farming, in others, it was peaches. In Habersham County, home of Cornelia, agents pushed the production of apples.

The agents became heroes when the boll weevil decimated Georgia's cotton crops, dropping output by 50 percent by 1924. Realizing that the apple had saved Habersham County from the destruction many counties experienced, the newly formed Kiwanis Club came up with the idea to honor the fruit with a statue.

Constructed of steel and concrete, the seven-foot statue

weighed in at 5,200 pounds. It was placed at the old train depot in downtown Cornelia, and dedication ceremonies were held on June 4, 1926. Nice story, huh?

Well, it ain't over yet. You see, yesterday's hero soon became today's villain. By 1932, the apple market had dropped drastically, leaving local farmers holding the bag (of apples). They placed the apples in storage, hoping for better prices that spring. But, alas, higher prices did not materialize, and now instead of just being out the cost of the crop, the farmers were out storage costs as well. The bumper crop that had saved the county just ten years ago now almost devastated it.

Cornelia's Big Red Apple honors the fruit that saved Habersham County from devastation.
Photo by Zeny Williams

Today, farming in Habersham County is pretty diversified, including apples, peaches, livestock, and catfish. But the Big Red Apple still holds its place of honor—and ignominy—in downtown Cornelia, where it's the focal point of the annual Fall Festival.

Located across from the intersection of U.S. 441 and the 129 Bypass.

GRINNING PEANUT • PLAINS

Does the grin on that big peanut look familiar? It should. It's the toothy smile of our thirty-ninth President. The thirteen-foot peanut—the world's second largest—was fashioned in 1976 by three Indiana residents when newly elected President Jimmy Carter was visiting the town of Evanston. To honor him these folks came up with the peanut idea for the town's planned parade. It's made from wooden hoops and chicken wire covered with aluminum foil and polyurethane. According to sculptor Loretta Townsend, the hole in the back of the peanut was ordered by the Secret Service. Gotta check for those bombs and other weapons of mass destruction, ya know.

Three Evanston Indiana residents built the Grinning Peanut in honor of President Jimmy Carter's visit, then sent it to Plains.
Courtesy of Plains Better Hometown Program

After the parade, the peanut was shipped to Plains, where for several years it was ravaged by souvenir hunters, who gouged out pieces to take home. Finally, the folks at the civic-minded, and advertising-gimmick savvy, Davis E-Z Shop rescued the peanut. Anchoring it with concrete, they planted it in front of the store, and restored and winterized it. It's definitely a sight to see.

Located on Highway 45.

Strange Statues

World Globe • Savannah

Imagination runs rampant in the family. Long before Ted Turner ever dreamed up that "All News All The Time" thing, father Robert was making his mark on Georgia. In 1956, he convinced Savannah's local gas company to paint a World Globe on their giant round gas storage tank. According to reports, the original artist must've skipped geography in school, for he painted the Land Down Under upside down.

The globe was repainted in 1999. Australia was righted and, in keeping with the coming millennium, the world was painted as if being viewed from space—with a hurricane headed straight for Savannah. This new artist must've missed some schooling, too, for at first the hurricane was pictured rotating clockwise, a mistake that was later corrected.

Located at the corner of White Bluff Road and 73rd Street.

- Peanuts rule! Georgia ranks No. 1 in the nation in peanuts, producing 1.3 billion pounds annually—45 percent of the nation's annual peanut yield.
- More than 80 counties in Georgia raise peanuts.
- More than 14,160 farms in Georgia raise peanuts.
- Georgia has approximately 250 peanut-related businesses.
- According to the Georgia Peanut Commission, Americans annually eat three pounds each of peanut butter.

Natural and Manmade Wonders

Wackiness abounds on the byways of our Strange But True Georgia. With its weird hodgepodge of natural and manmade wonders, you can visit a cloud forest and a rock city or contemplate the mysteries of the world at the South's own version of Stonehenge.

BRASSTOWN BALD • BLAIRSVILLE

At 4,784 feet, Brasstown Bald (aka Mt. Enotah) is Georgia's highest mountain. It's truly one of those purple mountain majesties, with a breathtaking panoramic view of four states.

Scientific explanations abound for the baldness of the mountain's summit—primeval upheaval, erosion—but we like the Cherokee version better. It says that the bald mountains exist because a horrible, sharp-clawed winged beast once lived on the mountaintop. This terrible, hungry beast would kidnap and eat little Native American children. The Cherokee cleared the forest from the summit and captured the beast. They then prayed to the Great Spirit, who killed the beast and kept the mountaintop clear of trees.

Because of the grass that covers the mountain's dome, the Cherokee named the mountain itse-yi, "new green place." It lost something in translation, though, when settlers misinterpreted the name as "untsaiyi," which means "brass."

One of the most interesting things about Brasstown Bald is its cloud forest, a type of rainforest found only in mountain areas. Low cloud banks form over the mountain and deposit large amounts of water onto the vegetation. In the highest elevations, the leaves are always dripping wet.

The mountain is festooned with hiking trails. There's also an archeological site containing three large boulders marked with ancient petroglyphs. Called degayelunha—the printed place—by the Cherokee, the stones are weathered, but their mysterious writings are still discernable.

A steep, paved trail leads from the parking lot to the Visitor Information Center, where you're greeted by an automaton of Arthur Woody, Georgia's first and most famous forest ranger, and another automaton of a more contemporary ranger. The two share the responsibility of educating you on the history and specifics of the mountain. Pretty freaky!

Located on the State Highway 180 Spur.

Georgia Guidestones • Elberton

Whoa, Nellie! Did you just somehow teleport over to England without realizing it? Nope. You're still in the good old U.S. of A. That's America's Stonehenge, better known as the Georgia Guidestones, you're seeing out there in that pasture. And if it's mystery you crave, then you're in the right place. There's as much mystery surrounding these monumental stones as the ones over there in that furren country.

The stones were commissioned from the Elberton Granite Finishing Company, Inc. by a mysterious stranger in 1979. Using the pseudonym R.C. Christian, the stranger said he represented a group that wanted to remain anonymous while erecting the monument as a guide to the conservation of mankind and the Earth.

The stones were to be carved and installed to exacting specifications. The maxims to be inscribed upon the stones were carefully worded and translated into eight languages, he said, as a moralistic appeal to all peoples of all nationalities, religions, and politics.

Photo by Zeny Williams

"Let These Be The Guidestones To The Age Of Reason" is inscribed around the edges of the capstone in Sanskrit, Babylonian Cuniform, Egyptian hieroglyphics, and classical Greek.

According to Christian, whose identity is still as unknown as the group he represented, Georgia was chosen for the monument because of the availability of excellent granite and its warm climate. The particular site—a former cow pasture—was chosen because it is the highest point in Elbert County, it commands a view to the East and West, and it's within the range of the summer and winter sunrises and sunsets.

Located on Highway 77.

Natural and Manmade Wonders

OK, maybe there's something to that positive energy thing with the Georgia Guidestones. Seems the Cherokee believed this area of North Georgia contained a special energy. They called it Ah-Yeh-Li A-Lo-Hee—The Center of The World. It was their official assembly ground, and they came here to worship and perform their tribal rituals. At Hartwell, on U.S. Highway 29, there's a granite marker that tells the story of the importance of the area.

GEORGIA STONEPILE • DAHLONEGA

Pass not by, Stranger! Stop! Silently bare your head, drop a stone upon her grave, and make a wish straight from your heart. The Spirit of Eternal Youth and Happiness hovers near to grant the wishes of all who love the hills and valleys of her native home.

This is the song of the Cherokee maiden Trahlyta, who loved the forest and mountains of her Georgia home—and with good reason. Legend has it that one day a wise Medicine Man told Trahlyta to walk along a path of that Georgia forest and she would come upon a spring. Drink from the spring, she was told, and she would become more beautiful with each sip. Of course, she did, and soon she became known for her incomparable beauty.

One day, along came the Cherokee warrior Wahsega, who, despite Trahlyta's rejection of his affections, vowed he would have her. He kidnapped her, spiriting her away to his land far away. Ignoring her pleas to return her to her beloved forest home, Wahsega cruelly watched as she slowly died of unhappiness. He did, however, grant her final wish to be buried on the mountain from which she had come. There, she said, strangers could drop a stone on her grave, and, they, too, may become young and beautiful, as she once was. "What they wish for shall be theirs!" she declared.

Through the years, the march of progress found Trahlyta's grave, but despite the fact that it lies in the path of road construction, it remains unmoved. Legend has it that twice an attempt was made to move the grave out of the path, but each time a fatal accident occurred. Bowing to the power of Trahlyta's spirit, the state decided to just work around it. The stonepile lies within a triangle between two intersecting roads.

Located at the intersection of U.S. Highway 19 and State Highway 60.

LITTLE WHITE HOUSE • WARM SPRINGS

During the late 1800s, Warm Springs was a resort where tired city dwellers came to be rejuvenated in the natural warm springs of the area. Word of the curative powers of the waters got around to Hyde Park resident Franklin D. Roosevelt, who, crippled by polio, had long searched for something that could help him regain use of his wasted legs.

Roosevelt began coming to Warm Springs in 1924, and he quickly noticed that while in the spring waters, he did, indeed, have better use of his legs. He consulted local physician Dr. James Johnson, and the two tried to understand the physical aspects of why swimming seemed to help. They never came to a conclusion, but did set the stage for later research and the establishment of hydrotherapy. Roosevelt went so far as to hold classes to guide other polio patients in the techniques that had helped him.

He was so enamored of the area that he spent two-thirds of his personal fortune to buy twelve thousand acres. Here, he established the Georgia Warm Springs Foundation, the country's first modern treatment center for infantile paralysis.

By 1932—the year he was elected president—Roosevelt was visiting Warm Springs so often that he finally built himself a home here. Dubbed the Little White House, the home doubled as a presidential retreat. He often entertained high-ranking officials and dignitaries here, and seeing first-hand the concerns of his rural neighbors, he conceived many of the New Deal programs that helped to bring the country out of the Great Depression.

Roosevelt was having his portrait painted at the Little White House on April 12, 1945, when he suffered a cerebral hemorrhage and died. It was his forty-first visit to Warm Springs.

The Georgia Warm Springs Foundation is now known as the Roosevelt Warm Springs Institute for Rehabilitation, and serves a wide variety of people with disabilities. The Little White House, where the unfinished portrait hangs, has been designated an historic site and is open to the public. In 1945, Elizabeth Shoumatoff completed a new portrait of Roosevelt, which hangs next to the unfinished one.

More than one hundred thousand annually take the tour, which includes visits to the guest house and the servant's quarters and garage. There is also an 11,000-square-foot museum containing many historical items.

Located at the intersection of U.S. Highway 27A and State Highway 85A.

> Blackbeard Island is so named because it was inhabited by pirate Edward "Blackbeard" Teach in the 1700s. The island was designated as a Wilderness Area in 1975. It encompasses three thousand acres.

PROVIDENCE CANYON • LUMPKIN

Wanna know how to make your own Grand Canyon? The folks around Lumpkin can tell ya.

Georgia's Providence Canyon, also known as Georgia Little Grand Canyon, was a fortuitous accident caused by both natural and manmade forces. It seems that in the 1800s, as settlers cleared trees in the area for cultivation, the loose soil began to erode. With little vegetation to stop it, rainwater washed away huge areas, resulting in three- to five-foot ditches by the 1850s. The pace of erosion only increased in the impoverished area after the Civil War, rapidly going from ditches to chasms in just a matter of years.

Today, there are nine canyons, ranging around 150 feet deep, 1300 feet long, and 600 feet across. Travel here, and you'll be treated to spectacular sunrises and sunsets glinting off the multi-hued layers of exposed rock.

Located on State Highway 39C, seven miles west of Lumpkin.

Natural and Manmade Wonders

PROVIDENCE SPRING HOUSE • ANDERSONVILLE

The summer of 1864 was hot and dry, and the tens of thousands of Union POWs incarcerated in Andersonville had only a small creek that was used as a drinking source, a laundry, and a latrine. You can imagine what kind of conditions they had to endure when the creek began to dry up.

Built in 1901, the Providence Spring House was erected over a natural spring that appeared after lightning struck the spot.
Courtesy of the National Park Service

No doubt, they all prayed for rain, and on August 13, their prayers were answered, big time. During the storm, a bolt of lightning supposedly struck the ground and up came a bubbling clear spring that washed away the creek's contamination. The spring still flows today.

The Providence Spring House was built over the spring in 1901 by the Women's Relief Corps. It can be visited at the Andersonville National Historic Site and Cemetery daily.

Located on Georgia Highway 49.

ROCK CITY • LOOKOUT MOUNTAIN

Rock City is one of the last surviving tourist attractions of a bygone era. Opened in 1932, it's a wonderful example of man's ability to kitsch up Mother Nature and turn the world into a billboard.

Even before the Civil War, the area had earned the name Rock City because of the immense boulder formations arranged as though to accommodate streets and lanes. Nearby, a 1,000-ton boulder balances atop two points of a small rock base, and the view from atop an outcropping called Lover's Leap affords a spectacular view of the 140-foot waterfall. Atop the mountain, you have a bird's eye view of seven states.

When Garnet and Frieda Carter came to Lookout Mountain in the 1920s, they took a look at all that natural beauty and thought…hmmm…needs a little something. Garnet was the consummate huckster, while Frieda had visions of fairies and gnomes dancing in her head. They bought seven hundred acres, which encompassed the Rock City area, and began construction on Fairyland, a residential neighborhood.

When construction on the planned golf course took longer than expected, Garnet, in an attempt to appease new residents, quickly built a Lilliputian course, now recognized as the first miniature golf course. The idea proved popular, and he began franchising his Tom Thumb golf courses across the nation.

Frieda, meanwhile, still had those visions of fairies and gnomes. Setting out a trail that wound through the unique rock formations and ended at Lover's Leap, she collected wildflowers and other plants and transplanted them beside her trail. All along the way, she placed statues of gnomes and famous fairy tale characters. Within a darkened cave, she fashioned Fairyland Caverns and Mother Goose Village, a wonderland of elves and gnomes and fairies and nursery rhyme characters. She covered the walls, floors, and ceilings of each underground room with sparkling crystals and fake stalagmites and stalactites. Garnet returned from his travels and said, "Hey, I can sell this!"

Rock City officially opened as a tourist attraction on May 21, 1932. To help draw in the masses and point the way to the mountaintop, Garnet hired Clark Byers, a young painter, to travel around the

At one time 900 See Rock City Barns were scattered throughout the country. Today only about 100 remain, including this one in Cumberland County, Tennessee.
Copyright David Jenkins

country, offering to paint farmers' barns for free. Well, almost for free. The catch was they had to agree to let him paint three words on the barn's roof: SEE ROCK CITY.

Byers was an industrious traveler, who for thirty years braved angry bulls, rain storms, and lightning bolts to climb the slippery barn roofs and paint his appointed message. Barns as far north as Michigan and as far west as Texas—and all points in between—soon sported Garnet's billboard. The advertising barns became a slice of true Americana, lining the highways of our youth. But, like our youth, the barns are quickly slipping away from us. Of the nine hundred original barns, only about one hundred remain, some of which have been designated as historic landmarks. As a marketing ploy, they were a huge success, drawing tourists in by the thousands. More than five hundred thousand annually, to be precise.

Come, see the wonders of Lookout Mountain, stuff yourself through Fat Man's Squeeze, and then purchase one of those cute little birdhouses as a memento of one of the country's most popular attractions.

Located at 1400 Patten Road.

ROCK EAGLE EFFIGY MOUND • EATONTON

The Rock Eagle Effigy Mound is a bit of a mystery. Experts aren't certain, but they think the mound, one of only two such mounds in the country (the other is also in Georgia), is the burial mound of the Woodland Indians, who inhabited the area from 1,000 BC to 1,000 AD.

First excavated in 1877, the mound measures 120 feet from head to toe and 102 feet wingtip to wingtip. It rises ten feet from the ground and is made from thousands of small- and medium-sized pieces of quartzite.

In the 1930s, the U.S. government bought the mound and the surrounding area and, utilizing the Works Progress Administration, built a granite stone tower at the foot of the effigy, giving a bird's eye view of the effigy—which is about the only way to really see it.

Today the effigy and the surrounding park is owned by the University of Georgia, which operates a natural history museum that includes information on the Woodland

Archaeologists speculate that Native Americans built the Rock Eagle Effigy Mound in the Middle Woodland Period about 2000 years ago.
Courtesy of the Rock Eagle 4-H Center

Indians and the Rock Eagle Effigy.

Located at 350 Rock Eagle Road.

"Georgia on My Mind," with music by Hoagy Carmichael and lyrics by Stuart Gorrell, was performed before a joint meeting of the Georgia Senate and House of Representatives on March 7, 1979, by Georgian Ray Charles. It was designated as Georgia's official state song on April 24 of that year.

Strange Museums

There's a strong sense of history here, as evidenced by the large number of museums throughout the state. But you won't find works by Picasso or Monet gracing these walls. Nah. We're much more interesting than that.

CARSON MCCULLERS HOUSE • COLUMBUS

Columbus must be a good place to breed talent. It's the home of novelist Carson McCullers, who spent her childhood here and returned to live out her later years.

Born Lula Carson Smith in 1917, she dreamed of becoming a concert pianist, but according to biographers, lost her music-school tuition in the New York subway, and somehow ended up studying writing at Columbia. She met and married Reeves McCullers, a soldier stationed at Ft. Benning, when she was twenty, and by all accounts it was a stormy marriage, with the couple divorcing and then remarrying.

When *The Heart Is A Lonely Hunter*, her first and possibly best, book, was published, McCullers was just twenty-three, a strange and gawky girl who wore men's clothing. She was sharing a house in New York with writers Richard Wright, Paul and Jane Bowles, composer Benjamin Britten, and stripper Gypsy Rose Lee.

Her personal life was tempestuous, marked by a destructive marriage, during which she reportedly engaged in several lesbian affairs, wild drinking, and partying. At age thirty, McCullers suffered a stroke, brought on because of misdiagnosed rheumatic fever as a child. She never regained her full strength or mobility, and for the next twenty years, she endured severe pain.

Reeves committed suicide in 1953, and Carson returned to Columbus, where she died from a massive stroke in 1967.

A historic marker stands in front of her childhood home at 1519 Stark Avenue.

DAHLONEGA COURTHOUSE GOLD MUSEUM • DAHLONEGA

There's gold in them thar hills! Sorry, it's cliché, but what else are you going to say when you're talking about America's first gold rush? That's right. The country's first gold rush happened in 1828, twenty years before California's big rush. And it happened right here in tiny Dahlonega (which is derived from the Cherokee word talonega meaning "golden").

It seems that ol' Benjamin Parks was out deer hunting one day when he tripped over a rock. Upon inspection, he found that rock was full of gold. GOLD!

The word spread quickly and more than fifteen thousand prospectors rushed to Dahlonega to make their fortune. Reportedly, the gold had been washing off the mountainsides for centuries. It was so plentiful that it just sat there on top of the ground, waiting to be picked up.

Mines sprang up and it was soon found that Dahlonega is home to a 22-inch thick gold-containing quartz vein, one of the largest in the world.

Two gold mines remain. Consolidated Gold Mines, built in the early 1900s, was once the largest gold mining operation east of the Mississippi. Daily tours are conducted by miners of the underground tunnel network, which, sixty feet below the Earth's surface, looks much as it did back in its heyday. Guides demonstrate mining techniques using early mining equipment, and for an extra fee (depending on how much you want to do), you can pan for your own gold. Located at 185 Consolidated Gold Mine Road.

Crisson Gold Mine dates back to 1847. Since this mine still ships gold to clients across the country, tours do not include the mine's tunnels. You can, however, see the operation of a 10-stamp mill, made in 1883, which was used to crush ore into sand-size particles so the gold could be separated by panning.

You can also pan for your own gold here and "grub" for gems, although it's a bit of a cheat, since the dirt containing the gems is shipped in from North Carolina. Keep your found gold for a souvenir or sell it to the Gold Shop in town. Located on U.S. Highway 19 Connector.

In your quest for riches, don't forget to stop by the Dahlonega Courthouse Gold Museum. The building was constructed in 1836 and is built with bricks containing small amounts of Georgia gold. You can learn the history of the Georgia gold rush, learn about mining techniques, and see gold nuggets and coins. Located in the Public Square.

Georgia Rural Telephone Museum • Leslie

Interested in the origins of that ubiquitous cell phone that just won't quit singing (Nobody has a plain old ring these days!)? Then visit the Georgia Rural Telephone Museum. Housed in a former cotton warehouse, the museum lays claims to "the world's largest collection of telephones and telephone memorabilia." The one-hour guided tour takes you through the entire history of the telephone. Exhibits include more than fifteen hundred phones, including candlestick phones, box phones, flip-top phones, and of course, the rotary dial phone. Don't miss the switchboard from the 1880s, manned by some Stepford-looking blonde mannequins, and the glass case containing all the Alexander Graham Bell phones. All this "telephony" history culminates with Bubba, the giant grizzly bear wearing an operator's headset. Children are urged to dial 1 on the nearby rotary phone (most will probably need instruction in this, since they've never seen a rotary phone) for a conversation with Bubba Bear.

Located at 135 North Bailey Avenue.

GERTRUDE RAINEY HOUSE • COLUMBUS

Known as the "Mother of the Blues," Gertrude "Ma" Pridgett Rainey grew up in Columbus, where she began her singing career at age fourteen by performing in *Bunch of Blackberries*, a local talent show. From there she began traveling in vaudeville and minstrel shows, where she met and married her husband, William "Pa" Rainey, in 1904.

For thirty years the Raineys toured with traveling minstrel shows, including F.S. Wolcott's *Rabbit Foot Minstrels* and *Tolliver's Circus and Musical Extravaganza*, where Ma played a central role in establishing the classic American blues.

A flamboyant personality, she captured attention the moment she walked onto the stage. Wearing her thick, coarse hair straightened and sticking out all over her head, she was a vision in gold—a sequined gown with a long triple-strand necklace sparkling with gold coins. Even her teeth were capped in gold. An ostrich plume in one hand topped off the outrageous outfit.

Her raspy, deep voice and moaning style held an emotional appeal for listeners. She was the first to incorporate blues into minstrel and vaudeville stage shows and was one of the first women to record the blues professionally. In her ninety-two recordings, Rainey was accompanied by such blues greats as Louis Armstrong,

Ma Rainey's Georgia Jazz Band was made up of "Gabriel," Albert Wynn, Dave Nelson, Ma, Ed Pollack, and Thomas A. Dorsey. Courtesy of the Georgia Music Hall of Fame and Museum

Lovie Austin, Buster Bailey, and Georgia Tom Dorsey. She is also known to have had a hand in developing the singing style of Bessie Smith, "The Queen of the Blues."

Rainey retired to Columbus in 1933, where she managed two theaters. She died in 1939, at a time when her work was beginning to gain serious notice among critics. It wasn't until 1983 that she was inducted into the Blues Foundation's Blues Hall of Fame. In 1990, she was inducted into the Rock 'n' Roll Hall of Fame and the Georgia Hall of Fame in 1992. The U.S.

Postal Service issued a stamp in her honor in 1994.

The Ma Rainey home is listed on the National Register of Historic Places and is commemorated with a plaque out front. Efforts are now underway to renovate the home and turn it into a museum.

Located at 805 Fifth Avenue.

GONE WITH THE WIND MUSEUMS • ATLANTA/ MARIETTA/ JONESBORO/ BARNESVILLE

Why, fiddle-dee-dee, suh! Did you think we'd forget about that little ol' movie *Gone With the Wind*? Nevuh! You won't either, after you take a tour through Scarlett O'Hara's Georgia.

There are no less than four museums devoted to the movie and book scattered across the state.

The Margaret Mitchell House and *Gone With the Wind* Museum in Atlanta is where Peggy Mitchell wrote her 1937 Pulitzer Prize-winning novel

Margaret Mitchell, author of the Pulitzer Prize winning *Gone with the Wind*, is remembered in several museums throughout Georgia.
Courtesy of Atlanta Historical Society

about the South. Mitchell said the theme of the book was survival. It was a study in what made some people capable of surviving catastrophe and what made others, just as strong, go under. "Gumption," she said, was what the survivors called it. "So, I wrote about the people who had gumption and the people that didn't."

Guess Missy Scarlett had the gumption, huh?

The guided tour takes you through the house Mitchell called "The Dump," where she lived while writing the book. You can see the window she gazed out as she pondered her story and learn the history of the vivacious writer, who began her career as a newspaper columnist for the *Atlanta Journal*. You can see it at 990 Peach Tree Street.

The museum is a look at the making of the movie, the movie itself, and life in Atlanta in December 1939, when the movie premiered there. Major attractions include the front door from Tara and the portrait of Scarlett that hung in the Butler mansion—complete with the stain of Rhett's thrown glass of bourbon. The museum also boasts of the world's largest collection of *Gone With the Wind* memorabilia.

Haven't seen the movie? Not to worry. At the *Gone With the Wind* Movie Museum in Marietta you can sit through it in its entirety—all four hours of it. Then tour the museum and see up close and personal many of the movie's items, most notably the Honeymoon Gown that Scarlett wore following her wedding to Rhett.

This museum also has a section devoted to Hattie McDaniel, who defied the NAACP to take the role of Mammy. As a result of her performance, McDaniel became the first African-American to win an Oscar.

Strange Museums

Jonesboro's Road to Tara Museum and Gift Shop is housed in the 1867 Jonesboro Depot Welcome Center. Here, you'll find original props from the movie, costume reproductions, a foreign edition library, and a photo gallery chronicling the making of the movie. Located at 104 North Main Street.

Not content with a few old items of memorabilia? Then visit the Tarleton Oaks Bed and Breakfast and the *Gone With the Wind* Hall of Stars Museum in Barnesville, owned and operated by actor Fred Crane, who played Brent Tarleton in the movie. Tarleton Oaks, an 1849 mansion, once served as a Confederate headquarters.

Here, you can stroll through the stately grounds, bonnet in hand, or curl up on the veranda with a mint julep and your copy of *GWTW*. Brent Tarleton, who spoke the first line in the movie, makes an appearance on your first night, with a slide show about *GWTW*. Guests are invited to peruse his private collection of *GWTW* items, including Margaret Mitchell's personal copy of the book, with her notations; personal items of Vivien Leigh, Clark Gable, and other *GWTW* stars; and autographed photos, costumes, and other memorabilia.

Take your time. Slow down. Immerse yourself in an era when time moved indolently through languid days. It matters not if you see all there is to see now. For, la, tomorrow's another day!

Located at 643 Greenwood Street.

LUNCH BOX MUSEUM • COLUMBUS

Designer jeans. Cell phones. Computers. Video games. All must-haves for kids today. We remember a simpler time. A time when the most coveted item was a Roy Rogers lunch box with a matching Roy Rogers thermos. (Yeah, OK, so now you know how old we are.) For more than thirty-five years, these popular fashion accessories were made of metal and decorated with the popular icons of the times. Then in 1986, the spoil-sport Florida legislature declared metal lunch boxes a lethal weapon—having been used to bean numerous kids on the skulls—and the industry discontinued the metal boxes in favor of those cheesy plastic ones.

If those metal boxes hold a special place in your heart, then stop in at the Lunch Box Museum, the world's largest such museum, where you'll find more than thirty-five hundred on display—some available for sale or trade. You'll find such baby boomer favorites as Lassie, the Lone Ranger, Matt Dillon, Popeye, and Mickey Mouse. There are also more contemporary ones, such as the Brady Bunch, The Bee Gees, and the Dukes of Hazzard. Ah, what childhood memories!

Located within the River Market Antiques and Art Center at 3226 Hamilton Road.

PANORAMIC ENCYCLOPEDIA OF EVERYTHING ELVIS • CORNELIA

Eww! When he was alive everyone wanted a piece of Elvis. Well, Joni Mabe's got a piece—maybe even two. Literally. Mabe's Panoramic Encyclopedia of Everything Elvis is recognized by the *Guinness Book of World Records* as the "largest and most unique Elvis exhibition in the world." The collection contains more than thirty thousand items, everything and anything Elvis. There are Elvis posters. Elvis lunch boxes. Elvis drawings. Elvis tapestries. Elvis love letters. Elvis record albums. Elvis T-shirts. ELVIS! ELVIS! ELVIS!

Without a doubt the grossest—and most prized—exhibits in Mabe's Kornucopia of the King are actual pieces of the man himself. Carefully preserved in a medical vial is Elvis's wart, which Mabe says she bought from the physician who removed it from Elvis's wrist. The vial is lovingly displayed in a red-velvet-lined box, with an accompanying photo of Elvis showing the offending wart.

The other piece of Elvis is just a maybe. When Mabe toured Graceland in 1983, she got down on her knees and rubbed the carpet—to get a feel where his sacred feet walked—and lo and behold, what does she find, but a hallowed toenail clipping! Hallelujah! It's a miracle! To have survived in that carpet for so long! Elvis died in 1977, ya know. Guess the housekeeping staff's been a bit lax since his demise. Anyway, Mabe makes no claim to certainty. She displays it as the "probably Elvis toenail clipping."

Even if you weren't much of an Elvis fan, you gotta see this. You certainly won't find anything much stranger. Thank you! Thank you, very much!

Located at 271 Foreacre Street.

Georgia's Okefenokee Swamp is the largest swamp in North America. The Okefenokee, which means Land of Trembling Earth in Seminole, is more than 700 square miles, crisscrossed by more than 120 miles of canoe trails. It provides sanctuary for hundreds of species of wildlife, including several endangered species.

SMITHSONIAN INSTITUTE TICK MUSEUM • STATESBORO

Double Ewww! OK, maybe this is at least as strange as Elvis's wart. The Smithsonian Institute Tick Museum houses the world's largest collection of ticks. The collection is nearly one hundred years old and contains more than seven hundred of the 850 known species of the nasty little bloodsuckers. You'll learn all about ticks and the diseases they carry. You'll see the largest and the smallest. And, as a special treat, you'll see the machine that freeze dries them and coats them with gold—all the better to see them with.

Located on the Georgia Southern University campus.

SOUTHERN FOREST WORLD MUSEUM • WAYCROSS

You may find this museum a bit, well, wooden. There is one thing, though, that makes the Southern Forest World Museum a must-stop on our Strange But True Georgia tour. Nope, it's not the animatronic talking tree or the endless displays of Southern forestry. Nope. Our reason for including this sleepy little museum is Stuckie the Petrified Dog. Stuckie (so dubbed in a recent naming contest) was discovered in the early 1980s by loggers clearing a stand of timber. It seems the unfortunate pooch was hunting with his master about forty years ago. He chased a raccoon into a hallow tree, and intent on catching his prey, wedged himself up into the tree, where he got stuck (Get it? Stuck, Stuckie?). Anyway, he died in that tree—no word on how come his master didn't cut down the tree and rescue him—and the conditions inside the tree preserved the carcass. The section of the tree containing Stuckie was donated to the museum, and it's become their most popular exhibit. Beats looking at the trees.

Located at 1450 North Augusta Avenue.

SOUTHERN MUSEUM OF CIVIL WAR AND LOCOMOTIVE HISTORY • KENNESAW

The Southern Museum of Civil War and Locomotive History houses an impressive collection of Civil War and railroad memorabilia. The most notable sight is the General, the locomotive that was stolen by Union spies and recovered by a band of brave Southerners. Visitors are treated to a movie about the chase and

The General, recovered during the Great Locomotive Chase, now rests at the Southern Museum of Civil War and Locomotive History.
Courtesy of Southern Museum of Civil War and Locomotive History

can view related exhibits. You'll also see the reproduction of the Glover Machine Works factory, the company most noted for helping to rebuild the South after the Civil War.

Located at 2829 Cherokee Street.

Who said it's just a state of good ol' boys? Georgia was the first state in the nation to allow women full property rights, and Wesleyan College in Macon was the first college in the world to grant degrees to women.

WESTVILLE LIVING HISTORY MUSEUM • LUMPKIN

Westville is a living history museum that depicts an 1850 Georgia village. More than thirty authentically furnished buildings are here, including homes, stores, workshops, churches, schools, and a courthouse. These historic buildings were moved to the site from around the state and carefully restored.

Your first stop here must be the Randle-Morton Store, which sells handicrafts made by village artisans. Since your modern day money is no good in the village, you'll need to trade for "scrip," in case you decide on a few purchases during your tour.

Stepping from the store, you find you've taken a huge step back in time. The townspeople, dressed in 1850s duds, go about their 1850s lives, using only the tools and equipment available in those days. You'll find a woodworking shop, an authentic blacksmith, a pottery making shop, candle making, quilting, and spinning and weaving.

As you wander through the village, passed by horse-drawn

wagons, you'll be riveted by the sights, sounds, and smells, especially the aroma of hearty hearth-cooked food, which you can purchase with your newly-acquired scrip.

The townsfolk are friendly, and if asked, they'll gladly tell you of their lives back in the day—when no one was just a phone call away, and when you said you were running out to the store, you really meant you were running. A day here is a good way to relive a bit of the past and find a new appreciation for our modern-day conveniences.

Located at 1850 Martin Luther King Jr. Drive.

THE WILLIAM WEINMAN MINERAL MUSEUM • CARTERSVILLE

The William Weinman Mineral Museum has hands-on exhibits. You can handle all the minerals you want, from silicates to oxides. Spellbinding, eh? Actually, those oxides are

The Weinman Mineral Museum features hands-on exhibits of minerals, gems, and fossils.
Courtesy of Weinman Mineral Museum

pretty cool, since they include rubies and sapphires. In addition to all manner of ore samples, the museum includes a simulated mine tunnel, waterfall, and a fossil room, and gold panning and fossil hunting are available.

Located at 51 Mineral Museum Drive.

WORLD OF COCA-COLA • ATLANTA

The World of Coca-Cola is a museum of sorts, honoring that most popular of soft drinks. You enter the building by passing under the "Neon Spectacular," an electronic billboard that from 1948 until 1981 graced Atlanta's Margaret Mitchell Square.

Inside the three-story atrium fly the flags of all two hundred countries where Coke is now sold. Take the giant glass elevators to the top floor and at your own pace tour the museum's galleries. There are more than 1,200 Coke-related artifacts to be seen. There are also interactive exhibits and video presentations, including a synopsis of world history as it pertains to Coke.

Did you know that five billion bottles of Coke were consumed by the U.S. military during WWII? And did you know that the Spanish-American War coincided with the opening of the first Coca-Cola bottling plant?

In "The Real Thing" gallery, you can take a nostalgic trip through the last forty years of Coca-Cola advertising. One marketing flub that's not mentioned is the Pepsi wannabe that was touted as New Coke. That formula bombed spectacularly, costing a few executives their jobs, no doubt, and proving that you shouldn't ought'a tinker with perfection.

You're going to be pretty thirsty after all that touring, so stop by the ultra high-tech soda fountain, where there's flashing neon, synthesized thunder booms, and mysterious bubbling brews in giant glass tanks, and where your soda selection shoots into your cup from a hidden high-pressure nozzle. Whew! And don't forget to stop by the gift shop on the way out for those nifty Coca-Cola souvenirs!

Presently located at 55 Martin Luther King Jr. Drive— across from Underground Atlanta but is scheduled to move to Atlanta's Centennial Park in 2006.

The "Neon Spectacular" marks the entrance to the World of Coca-Cola.
Photo by Jacquie Wansley

Coca-Cola was invented by Atlanta's Dr. John Pemberton in Atlanta, Georgia, in May 1886. His bookkeeper, Frank Robinson, suggested the name "Coca-Cola," and wrote it in the script that remains the famous trademark even today. The drink was first sold at Jacob's Pharmacy in Atlanta by Willis Venable.

Weird Roadside Attractions

ATLANTA CYCLORAMA • ATLANTA

Just in case you are wondering, a cyclorama is a large panoramic painting placed on the walls of a cylindrical room. Placing it so gives the viewer a feeling of being in the midst of the action. The rage in eighteenth and nineteenth century Europe, they often depicted Napoleonic battles or the splendors of ancient Rome.

The Atlanta Cyclorama depicts the bloody Battle of Atlanta, which, of course, ended with Sherman burning the city to its cobblestones. The painting was commissioned in 1886 by Yankee General John Logan as part of his unsuccessful campaign bid for the Vice Presidency.

Since it's a Yankee-commissioned painting, it depicts much Union heroism, and no one figures in more heroically than General John Logan himself. Originally called "Logan's Great Battle," the painting features Logan astride his fiery steed, braving enemy fire to lead his soldiers into the battle.

Anyway, some nitpickers say Logan's part in the battle was nowhere near as glorious as depicted in the cyclorama, but it was his picture, by golly, and he could paint it any way he wanted. It took eleven German artists to complete the fifty-foot high, 400-foot long painting. When finished it weighed more than nine thousand pounds.

When Logan lost the VP race, he stuck his lip out and sold the painting to a traveling circus, which somehow ended up in

Weird Roadside Attractions

Atlanta. Well, as you might imagine, not many of Atlanta's good citizens cared to view that Yankee picture. They stayed away in droves. The circus went bankrupt and sold both the painting and the animals to lumber merchant George Gress. He used the animals to start Grant Park Zoo—now Zoo Atlanta—and installed the cyclorama in a wooden building next to it.

The Atlanta Cyclorama is still housed next to the zoo, but now it inhabits a state-of-the-art facility, designed to preserve the delicate painting. Because of an $11 million restoration to repair damage incurred in its circus travels, the cyclorama now measures 42' x 358', still the world's largest painting. The fact that it's been on display since 1893 makes it the country's longest running show. A video of the historic battle—in which the Confederacy lost eight thousand soldiers and the Union lost thirty-seven hundred—precedes your viewing of the painting.

Housed within the same building is the Atlanta Civil War Museum, which contains two floors of Civil War artifacts, including weapons, photographs, and uniforms. The museum's centerpiece is the Texas, the locomotive that recaptured the purloined General in the Great Locomotive Chase.

Located at 800 Cherokee Avenue Southeast in Grant Park.

ATLANTA FED • ATLANTA

The Federal Reserve Bank of Atlanta, casually known as the Atlanta Fed, has come up with a fun idea: Hey, let's educate folks on all that money they're spending! At its Visitor Center and Monetary Museum, you can learn everything there is to know about the green stuff. There's a comprehensive history of money, told through an exhibit of artifacts from gold nuggets to wampam to modern currency. The Fed's importance to monetary policy and the economy are discussed, and you can visit the bank's money processing center "where millions of dollars are counted, sorted, and shredded daily." This isn't one of those hands-on exhibits, though. So forget trying to palm a few of those bills before they hit the shredder. We're just hoping Fed's financial wizards can explain to us how our bank account can be overdrawn when we still have checks left!

Located at 1000 Peachtree Street Northeast.

BABYLAND GENERAL HOSPITAL • CLEVELAND

Freaky. There's no other way to describe the Babyland General Hospital. Remember Cabbage Patch dolls, the biggest craze of the '80s? Ugly little soft dolls that were supposedly born in a cabbage patch and that you couldn't just buy, you had to "adopt"? No? Well, apparently some people still remember them. Some even take yearly pilgrimages to the hospital to see the new crop of pudgy-faced babies and pay big money to adopt one or two more. Freaky.

At Babyland General Hospital, you can adopt your own Cabbage Patch doll.
Photo by Zeny Williams

Babyland General Hospital is located in a building that once housed a turn-of-the-century medical clinic. Looking like something from a Wes Craven movie, it's set up to resemble a maternity hospital and is staffed by LPNs (License Patch Nurses) and doctors. There's a nursery for the newborns and incubators for the preemies.

The delivery room is quite a trip. The giant Magic Crystal Tree stands in the center, with Bunnybees, a less popular type of Cabbage Patch kid, hanging from the boughs. Underneath, the heads of little Cabbage Patch kids poke from cabbages.

Suddenly you hear, "Code Green! Cabbage dilation!" An LPN emerges from the tree's trunk to examine the mother cabbage—which she announces is dilated a full ten leaves. Reaching into the cabbage, she withdraws the baby Cabbage Patch, and wraps it in a blanket. Announcing the baby's sex, she asks the audience for a name, then announces it will be up for adoption in the Babyland nursery. Double freaky.

Of course, there's also a gift shop, where you can adopt all the Cabbage Patch Kids you want. May not be able to afford many, though. You'd think after a craze was over, the price would drop. Not so. Little Cabbage Patch Kids that once sold for $30 go for more than $200 these days. Go figure.

Located at 73 West Underwood Street.

CENTER FOR PUPPETRY ARTS • ATLANTA

Always wanted to pull a few strings? Then the Center For Puppetry Arts is the place for you. The center opened in 1978 as the country's first puppetry center, and today, is the largest center dedicated to the puppetry arts in the U.S.

The hands-on museum displays more than 350 puppets from around the world. Tours include the Puppet Storage Room, where puppets cover the walls, ceilings, and floors. Don't freak out if you see them move—several throughout the room are electronically controlled. There's also a Behind-The-Scenes tour, where you can see how puppets are made. If you have a little time on your hands, you can sign up for one of the

Pavakathakali, a hand puppet, is featured in PUPPETRY IN FOCUS: Treasures from the Global Collection at the Center for the Puppetry Arts. Photo by Bradford Clark

workshops, where for a little while you can channel Geppetto.

Located at 1404 Spring Street Northwest.

WILDER TOWER • FORT OGLETHORPE

OK. Here's a Strange But True Georgia attraction. A Yankee memorial slap dab in the Heart of Dixie! Wilder Tower was built to honor the men of the Union's Lightning Brigade who died in the Battle of Chickamauga and their leader, Colonel John T. Wilder.

The circular tower was begun in 1892, mostly paid for by Wilder's men. A bank failure and subsequent loss of funds in 1893 ended work on the tower when it was a mere sixty feet tall. Work resumed in 1897, but it was 1904 before the 85-foot tower was completed. In 1915, the tower took a direct hit from lightning, damaging the top and interior staircase, but it was quickly repaired. The tower was rededicated on

The Wilder Tower honors the Yankee troops who died in the Battle of Chickamauga.
Photo by Eric Long/Chickamauga and Chattanooga National Military Park

June 8, 1963, by a group of Civil War Centennial Commissioners from Indiana, the first monument on the Chickamauga battlefield to be rededicated.

Located within the Chickamauga Battlefield.

WORLD'S SMALLEST CHURCH • SOUTH NEWPORT

The World's Smallest Church (one of fifteen to make this claim) is 10' x 20' and is complete with tiny pews, pulpit, and even a stained glass window. The church is active, and visitors are welcome.

Located on Highway 17.

The Haunting of Georgia

Mist rising on moonlit nights. Ghostly apparitions floating through hallowed halls. Strange and scary noises. Georgia can be a spooky place at night. With a past so rich in history, it's no wonder there are haints wandering this land. Here's just a smattering of Georgia's legendary ghost tales.

ANTHONY'S RESTAURANT • ATLANTA
Everyone's a food critic. At Anthony's Restaurant, a mansion built in 1797, dishware has been known to fly across the room on its own volition. Strange voices can be heard, and some have reported the strong feeling of a hand placed upon the back — mostly attractive women, we suppose!

Ghost hunting won't be your only treat at Anthony's. It's considered one of the best steakhouses in Atlanta—and that's saying a lot. Don't worry if you feel a tap on your shoulder, though, and find no one there. It's just the resident ghost telling you to mind your manners.

Located at 3109 Piedmont Road.

ASHFORD MANOR • WATKINSVILLE
Some pretty strange things began happening at Ashford Manor when it was purchased by three businessmen from up North who planned to turn it into a bed and breakfast. Until then, the home had been owned by the Ashford family since it was built in 1893. The first night the men stayed in the house, they heard a loud

crash, and upon investigation found that a chandelier arm had mysteriously broken. During renovation, all three men reported a constant strong feeling of being watched, and one of the carpenters sighted a man walking through one of the rooms, when no one was in the house.

Further investigation found that A.W. Ashford had died in that room after the stock market crash of 1929. It might have been he. Then again it could have been the (unnamed) murder

A stay at Ashford Manor Bed & Breakfast could result in the eerie feeling of being watched. Courtesy of Ashford Manor Bed & Breakfast

victim who died in that same room after having been stabbed.

Located at 5 Hardin Hill Road.

THE BONAVENTURE CEMETERY • SAVANNAH

Despite its Southern gentility, Savannah has a violent and tragic past. It was a battleground in the American Revolution, was captured by Sherman during the Civil War, and has weathered hurricanes, fires, and two devastating yellow fever epidemics. It's no wonder, then, that this picturesque river town is known as The Most Haunted City In America.

The Bonaventure Cemetery is one of Savannah's most haunted spots. Some well-known spirits wander this American Revolution-era cemetery, where patriots, soldiers, and artists are buried.

Located at 330 Bonaventure Road.

THE BRIDGE ON METROPOLITAN AVENUE • ATLANTA

The Bridge on Metropolitan Avenue is said to be haunted by a young lady in white. Supposedly, the lady will flag for a ride home. If you give her a ride to her home (no word on just what that address is), she gets out of the car, thanks you for the ride, and promptly vanishes. Now, if you go to the door, just to be sure the young lady made it inside, an older woman comes to the door and explains that people are always dropping her daughter off. Seems the young lady in white was killed in an auto accident ten years before. (Insert *Twilight Zone* music here.)

Located on Metropolitan Avenue by University Street.

THE CHICKAMAUGA BATTLEFIELD • FORT OGLETHORPE

The Chickamauga Battlefield is a really spooky place, with good reason: More than thirty-four thousand soldiers died in the Battle of Chickamauga, a Confederate victory. It's said that every night an eerie fog rolls onto the battlefield. The fog is seen only on the battlefield. There are also reports of sightings of an apparition called "Green Eyes," supposedly a Confederate soldier who was killed in the battle by his Yankee twin brother. It seems his eyes glow green in the night, as the ghost floats down Snod Grass Hill. If he sees you, and you look into his glowing eyes, he will stare you down until you run screaming into the night.

There is another tale of a bride-to-be wandering the battlefield in her bedraggled wedding dress, looking for her lost fiancé, who died there.

Monuments in Viniard Field mark Union and Confederate efforts on the haunted Chickamauga Battlefield.
Photo by Eric Long/Chickamauga and Chattanooga National Military Park

Located one at 3370 Lafayette Road.

CHRIST CHURCH CEMETERY • ST. SIMON'S ISLAND

Drive past Christ Church Cemetery on a dark night and you may see a light moving through the headstones. According to legend, there was a young wife who was terribly afraid of the dark. When she died, her husband, distraught at the thought of her sleeping in the dark, kept a candle on her grave. Some say that today he still lights her grave with the mysterious light.

Located at 101 12th Street.

THE COGDELL LIGHT • ATKINSON

The Cogdell Light is a popular haunt on the fringe of the Okefenokee Swamp. According to legend, you can drive into the woods, turn off the car, and flash the headlights a time or two. If you've timed your visit just right, you'll see an eerie green glow coming toward you from the dank swamp.

There are two stories surrounding the mysterious light. Some say it's the ghost of a man who was decapitated in a train accident. He's swinging a lantern in search of his missing head—how he's gonna see it, we don't know. The other story concerns two star-crossed lovers whose parents forbade them to see each other. They planned to flag down the train with a lantern and elope. Unfortunately, the girl's father shot them, thinking they were prowlers. The green glow is supposedly the light of their lantern. Huh.

We have just two words for ya: SWAMP GAS.

THE HAMPTON LILLIBRIDGE HOUSE • SAVANNAH

Said to be the most haunted house in Savannah, the Hampton Lillibridge House was one of the few to survive the great 1820 fire. The house was moved to its present site in the 1960s by owner Jim Williams, who was later tried three times for the murder of his associate. The trials inspired the book—and subsequent movie—*Midnight in the Garden of Good and Evil*. During the restoration of the house, a worker was killed when an adjacent building collapsed. After that, strange things started happening. One workman was found clinging to an upstairs floor, convinced that some strange force was trying to pull him through an opening in the floor—a thirty-foot drop. Workmen began walking off the job, reporting disappearing tools, strange footsteps, eerie feelings, and once, the sighting of a man wearing a black suit and bow tie. Neighbors also heard a woman's screams coming from the house. Because of these occurrences, Williams had the house exorcised by a bishop of the Episcopal diocese of Savannah on December 7, 1963.

The exorcism may have rid the house of those early ghosts, but there are more recent reports of the house being haunted by Williams, who had become famous for the opulent parties he threw on the same night every year. Years after his death, there are ongoing reports of lights and the sounds of festivities in the mansion on the same night of the year of Williams' party. Bet all those spectral revelers felt like death warmed over the next day!

Located at 507 East Julian Street.

THE HAY HOUSE • MACON

The Hay House, built by entrepreneur William Johnson in 1855, was a house ahead of its time. The twenty-room mansion had indoor plumbing with hot and cold running water—in a time when outhouses with

Built in 1855, the Hay House has had many owners, some who decided to spend eternity there.
Courtesy of The Georgia Trust

little carved moons on the door were all the rage. He also had a ventilation system to heat and cool the house and an elevator.

Johnson's daughter sold the home to Parker Lee Hay, the local banker, in 1926. The family owned it until 1962, when it was converted into a museum and subsequently donated to the Georgia Trust for Historic Preservation.

A couple of the home's former owners have found the house more comfortable than their final destinations, it seems. There are reports of an elderly woman, a former owner, roaming the halls, and further reports of mysterious phantom footsteps, cold spots on the grand staircase, and moaning coming from the master bedroom.

Located at 934 Georgia Avenue.

HERITAGE HALL • MADISON

Heritage Hall is a stately mansion built in 1811 by a prominent physician. On two separate occasions, visitors in a certain room, now known as the Ghost Room, claim to have seen the apparition of a young

The hearth of Heritage Hall holds the image of three figures that the strongest cleaner cannot erase.
Photo by Sarah Maugliani

woman in bed holding a baby. A servant woman was kneeling at the foot of the bed. Both visitors say they had the strong feeling that a tragedy had occurred here. There supposedly is the outline of three figures on the hearth in this room that no amount of cleaning will remove, and there are reports of a baby crying in the night.

Located at 227 South Main Street.

JEKYLL ISLAND CLUB AND HOTEL • JEKYLL ISLAND

The exclusive Jekyll Island Club and Hotel was a favorite haunt of Southern Railroad Company President Samuel Spencer. Every morning he requested that the *Wall Street Journal* be delivered directly to his room,

Newspapers and coffee cups at the Jekyll Island Club Hotel move at the hand of former guest Samuel Spencer.
Courtesy of the Jekyll Island Club Hotel

so that he could peruse it with his morning coffee. Spencer was killed in 1906, ironically in a tragic train accident, but the club remains one of his favorite haunts.

Seems he still enjoys a cup of coffee with his morning paper. Frequently guests and members occupying Spencer's old room report finding their newspapers moved or folded in their absence and their coffee cup poured or moved in some way.

Located at 371 Riverview Drive.

THE JULIETTE GORDON LOW BIRTHPLACE • SAVANNAH

Juliette Gordon Low, the founder of the Girl Scouts of America, was born and raised in Savannah. Her family home is supposedly haunted by two former owners: her mother, Nellie, and her grandmother, Sarah. Objects in the house disappear and reappear and furniture is often rearranged. Nellie liked to play the piano, and ghostly music can sometimes be heard late at night. The home's

The mother and grandmother of Juliette Gordon Low, founder of the Girl Scouts, continue to haunt her birthplace.
Courtesy of the Juliette Gordon Low Birthplace

maintenance man says that on many mornings when he arrives for work, he sees Nellie, wearing a blue robe with flowers, sitting at the breakfast table. Others have reported seeing Sarah wandering the hallways in a long, old-fashioned dress.

Located at 10 East Oglethorpe Avenue.

THE KEHOE HOUSE • SAVANNAH

Built in 1892, the Kehoe House is a well-known haunted house. The ghostly presences seem to have an affinity for rooms 201 and 203. The spirit of a woman has been sighted, accompanied by the strong scent of roses.

Located at 123 Habersham Street.

The Haunting of Georgia

THE MARSHALL HOUSE • SAVANNAH

Built in 1851, the Marshall House was Savannah's first hotel. During the Civil War, between 1864 and 1865, it was occupied by General Sherman's troops and served as a Union hospital, a fact that has come back to haunt today.

During a recent restoration of the building, which is still one of Savannah's premiere hotels, the workmen performing structural checks in the building's crawl space had to keep tossing aside objects that they assumed to be rocks. Finally, someone took the time to shine a light on these "rocks" only to discover that

During renovations to Marshall House, amputated body parts were found hidden in storage spaces.
Courtesy of Marshall House

they were human bones—most specifically, arm and leg bones. It seems back in the time of the Civil War, amputation was the only treatment for badly damaged limbs. The amputated parts were simply pitched underneath the house like so much garbage. The ghosts of these wounded soldiers are said to roam the third floor of the hotel...searching for something, perhaps?

Located at 123 East Broughton Street.

THE OLD GOVERNOR'S MANSION • MILLEDGEVILLE

The Old Governor's Mansion is haunted by Molly, who spent her life cooking there, and it seems she's still at it. Delicious aromas emanate from the basement, which is where the kitchen was once located. Ghostly apparitions have been seen, and footsteps are often heard coming up the stairs.

A former cook haunts the kitchen of the Old Governor's Mansion. Photo by Tim Vacula, Georgia College & State University

Located at 120 South Clarke Street.

PANOLA HALL • EATONTON

Built in 1854, Panola Hall is haunted by Sylvia, the snobby ghost. Supposedly, the lovely, dark-haired Sylvia will appear only to those she considers her social equals. One such lucky gentleman who says he passed Sylvia on the stairway of Panola Hall reported the scent of Damask Roses in her hair.

Located at 400 North Madison Avenue.

The Haunting of Georgia

PIRATE'S HOUSE RESTAURANT • SAVANNAH

Originally a sailor's pub in the 1700s, The Pirate's House Restaurant is said to be haunted by pirates Captain Redbeard and Captain Flint from Robert Louis Stevenson's *Treasure Island*.

OK—Redbeard we might buy. According to legend, with the Savannah River just a block away, the pub was a hub of bloodthirsty pirate activity. In the chamber that is now known as the Captain's Room, clandestine negotiations were made with understaffed ship captains to shanghai men for pirate

The Pirate's House Restaurant is supposedly haunted by Captain Redbeard and the fictional Captain Flint. Courtesy of Spectrum Printing & Marketing, Inc.

excursions via a tunnel extending from the pub's wine cellar to the Savannah River. Many a civilian drank himself into oblivion and awoke the next day aboard a strange ship bound for the Caribbean. In one most notable legend, a Savannah policeman was shanghaied from the pub, where he'd stopped for a quick grog, and awoke on a schooner headed to China. It took him two years to get back home. What with all that shanghaiing, fighting, and bloodthirstiness going on, it's no wonder that a few discontent pirate haints might be wandering the pub.

We don't believe Captain Flint is among them, however. According to the official restaurant history, the pub is mentioned several times in *Treasure Island* and, in fact, they say, some of the book's action took place here. In their version, Captain Flint supposedly died in an upstairs room of the pub— uttering his last words "Darby, fetch aft the rum." Even now, they say, many believe the ghost of Captain Flint haunts the Pirate's House on moonless nights. Hey! Great story, huh? Just one little nitpicky point: Captain Flint was a figment of RLS's imagination, so anyone sighting him must have a pretty vivid imagination as well!

Located at 20 East Broad Street.

17 HUNDRED 90 INN AND RESTAURANT • SAVANNAH

Built in 1790, this inn is said to be haunted by the spirit of Anna Powell, a seventeen-year-old girl who, in the early 1800s, had the misfortune to fall in love with a sailor. According to legend, Anna watched from the third floor balcony of the inn as the sails of her lover's ship left the harbor. So distraught was she—certain that he would never return—that she jumped from the balcony onto the brick courtyard below.

Since her death, guests and employees have reported strange goings on throughout the inn, especially in room 204, Anna's room. Neighbors tell of seeing Anna sitting on the veranda, and there have been reports of chairs rocking, windows opening, and stairs making noise. One couple said that they returned to their room to find it mysteriously locked from the inside. After several attempts to open it, they fetched the manager, for whom the door readily opened.

Located at 307 East President Street.

SHAKESPEARE TAVERN • ATLANTA

Advertised as a place to eat, drink, and nourish the soul, this Shakespeare theater seems to be inhabited by more than just a few lost souls. In 1993, the actor playing Falstaff in a production of *Henry IV* was shaken by the appearance of a young boy dressed in a circa 1800s velvet suit. Others have reported seeing

A young boy, a female figure, and maybe even old Will himself are a few of the spirits frequenting the Shakespeare Tavern.
Photo by Jeff Watkins

an old man wandering the halls (maybe old Will himself?). A female figure has also been seen. She often upsets objects in the women's dressing room during performances. Huh, everyone's a critic.

Located at 449 Peachtree Street Northeast.

THE ST. SIMON'S LIGHTHOUSE • ST. SIMON'S ISLAND

This lighthouse is one of the oldest working lighthouses in the country. In the dead of night, the clump of ghostly footsteps can be heard on the lighthouse staircase. Some say it's a former tender coming to check on the light.

SURRENCY GHOST LIGHT • SURRENCY

A minor domestic dispute is the story behind the Surrency Ghost Light. According to the

St. Simon's Lighthouse, one of the oldest working lighthouses, is said to be haunted by a former tender. Courtesy of the Coastal Georgia Historical Society

story, a couple who lived near the town's railroad tracks had an argument one night. Upset, the woman ran from the house and down the tracks, where she was hit and killed by a train. Today, witnesses report seeing a lantern light moving along the tracks—the man searching for his wife, they say. There also have been sightings of a ghostly lady with long blonde hair walking along the tracks. The locals have dubbed her the Blue Lady.

THE TELFAIR MUSEUM • SAVANNAH

Better be on your best Ps and Qs here. This museum, the oldest art museum in the South, was once the Telfair home, built in 1818. The house and its furnishings were bequeathed to the Georgia Historical Society in 1875 by owner Mary Telfair, with a few stipulations: allow no alcoholic beverages or smoking, and for heaven's sakes, take care of the furniture! To ensure that the new proprietors followed her admonitions to the letter, Miss Mary decided to hang around awhile—oh, a hundred years or so. Try to

Former owner Mary Telfair is said to wander the halls of the Telfair Museum of Art.
Courtesy of Telfair Museum of Art

smoke a cigarette in the house or sit on the wrong chair, and you'll hear angry footsteps headed your way. She's also been sighted wandering the halls in a long, flowing dress.

Located at 121 Barnard Street.

TUNNEL HILL • TUNNEL HILL

Tunnel Hill is reported to be one of the most haunted places in Georgia. The area is the site of no less than four major Civil

War battles, so it's no wonder that strange things are reported there on a regular basis. There are accounts of bloodcurdling screams, phantom campfires, ghostly apparitions, and the sickening smell of rotting flesh.

Battle reenactments are held here annually, and reenactors report frequent spooky encounters. They report standing next to Confederate soldiers they believe to be fellow reenactors, only to have them disappear before their eyes. Several have reported seeing phantom campfires, with ghostly hands reaching toward them for warmth. When the reenactors approach, the campfires disappear, only to return when they walk away.

THE UNIVERSITY OF GEORGIA CAMPUS • ATHENS

The UGA campus is said to be haunted by ousted student Robert Toombs. After his humiliation at UGA, Toombs must've straightened up and flown right. He went on to become an honored lawyer, a U.S. Senator, and a highly decorated Confederate soldier. Perhaps he returns to the UGA campus to relive the misspent days of youth. Whatever the reason, many students have reported seeing a man dressed in a Confederate uniform standing outside Demosthenian Hall.

The reports of ghostly happenings are so numerous in Georgia that there are eight paranormal research teams to check them out: The Georgia Ghost Society, The Georgia Haunt Hunt Team, The Foundation for Paranormal Research, The Georgia Paranormal Research Center, Inc., GhostForce, Georgia Paranormal Research Team, and Northwest Georgia Paranormal Investigation Team. Need a little ghost busting done? So now ya know who to call.

Weird Encounters of the Georgia Kind

Hairy men traipsing around the countryside. Really, really big pigs hiding in the swamps. Spacemen traversing the heavens. There are weird things happening here.

Big Foot

There's a hairy creature inhabiting the forests and swamps of Georgia, and no, it's not your Uncle Buddy off on a toot. Might be Aunt Thelma, though. This creature is about seven feet tall, is sheepdog hairy, and has a face that would stop a clock. Got big feet, too. Wears about a size 52. And it always causes a big stink. Yep, that's Auntie T, all right.

Then again, it could be Georgia's Big Foot, also sometimes known as the Georgia Swamp Ape. Reports of the creature have been around for decades and have come from the North Georgia mountains to the South Georgia swamps. In fact, Georgia's Pike County is the site of what's been called by experts "the best evidence of Big Foot's existence in the Eastern United States."

This evidence is a giant footprint, cast by Pike County sheriff's deputy James Akins in 1997. The print, found along Elkins Creek after reports of strange happenings in the area, is 17.5" long and 8.5" wide. The cast is unique, experts say, because it picked up "dermal ridges," the foot's equivalent of fingerprints.

Weird Encounters of the Georgia Kind

The ridges in this footprint lacked the tension seen in human prints, and instead, resembled those of an ape. Upon further study, it was found that the particular ridge patterns did not occur in humans or any known primates. They did, however, resemble the patterns found in two Big Foot prints cast in the Northwest. Yankee cousins, perhaps?

If Big Foot hunting is of interest, then Georgia might just be the place. The hirsute creature is not coy here, revealing himself on a regular basis (another resemblance to Auntie T). Here are just a few Georgia sightings (of Big Foot, not Aunt Thelma).

ATHENS

In 1971, two Clarke County sheriff's deputies responded to a suspicious prowler call at a local business. When they stepped from their patrol car, they immediately noticed a powerful stink in the area. They had been there only a few minutes when they sighted a seven-foot creature standing in the darkness.

AUGUSTA

In 1979, Jack Hovatter, a retired military man, was hunting in the woods on Fort Gordon Army Base when he found a large footprint leading into what he at first thought was an impenetrable thicket. Seeing a path inside, he stepped into the brush and was suddenly rushed by an apelike creature thickly covered in hair that looked ten-feet tall. It wasn't vicious, he said, but it did mean business, and though he was armed, Hovatter said his 16-gauge shotgun seemed like a .22. He slowly backed from the thicket and the creature didn't follow.

BLUE RIDGE

Is the plural of Big Foot, Big Feet? Dunno, but here's a plural report. In 1999, a glassworker arrived at a mountain cabin to take measurements for windows. Standing on the cabin's balcony was not one, but two, hmmm…Big Foots? One was gray and was seven-foot tall. The other was brown and was just a bit smaller.

The creatures calmly walked down the stairs and strolled off into the woods. Upon investigation, the glassworker found a pile of sticks and old clothing in a room that appeared to be bedding.

CUSSETA

A woman walking along a rural road in the early evening reported a thudding sound, as if something heavy was walking in the woods along the road. There was also an unpleasant odor hanging in the air. Oh, wait. That was Aunt Thelma. Must've been out searching for Uncle Buddy.

EFFINGHAM COUNTY

One morning before dawn in 1976, a man riding his motorcycle to work saw something run from the woods and stop on the side of the road. Afraid it would run out in front of him, he stopped his bike and turned the headlight toward the creature. It was a seven-foot, big hairy thing. The creature watched him, lowering its head as if to look underneath the headlight, then turned and bolted back into the swamp.

Weird Encounters of the Georgia Kind

Franklin County

In 1988, a father and his two young sons were riding down a rural road in the dead of night, when an animal that they were sure was a wolf ran across in front of them. A few seconds later, an eight-foot tall manlike creature covered in shaggy, grayish-brown hair ran across. It looked over its shoulder at the pickup, then gracefully hurdled a four-foot barbed wire fence. Running about thirty yards, it then stopped and turned to face the truck, its eyes glowing a strange amber color. It watched the truck for several moments, then turning, it ran off with the wolf following behind. They also noted a nasty smell, a mixture between "a dead animal, a dirty dog, and sewage."

Okefenokee Swamp

Guess this is where Big Foot becomes known as the Swamp Ape. In 1972, a fourteen-year-old boy walking along a waterway in Stephen Foster State Park heard footsteps behind him. Thinking his siblings were trying to sneak up on him, he stepped off the path to wait for them. A few moments later, says the boy, "a thing that looked like a cross between a chimpanzee and a little man," came sauntering down the path. When it caught sight of the boy, it let out an unearthly scream and jumped on him. Knocking him to the ground, it tried to bite him, but ran away when the boy screamed.

There've been two other notable sightings in the swamp. Two farmers hunting deer near Waycross reported seeing a seven-foot tall creature covered in brown hair crossing the railroad tracks. It stopped for a moment and stared at the men, then continued on its way.

Several years ago, a family visiting their Granny, who lived near the swamp, were fishing. Suddenly, a big, hairy apelike creature stepped from the woods, grabbed their stringer of fish, and took off. The father gave pursuit, but fled when the creature turned and screamed at him.

Hogzilla

This must be Big Foot's barbecue. Reports of a giant hog, nicknamed Hogzilla by locals, had floated around the area for many years. Some believed. Most did not. The believers won out in 2004, when local hunting guide Chris Griffin finally brought home the bacon.

Hogzilla was bagged on an Alapaha hunting preserve owned by Ken Holyoak, who said the hog weighed one thousand pounds and measured twelve feet. A photo of Griffin, dwarfed by the animal hanging upside down from a backhoe, caused much controversy on the Internet. Some believed it to be a hoax, perpetrated by trick photography.

"Not so!" says *National Geographic*, who sent a team to investigate. The team exhumed the pig corpse and after allowing for desiccation, calculated that the big pig actually weighed around eight hundred pounds and measured around eight feet. Holyoak begs to disagree—he weighed and measured the pig himself and says his measurements were true.

Either way, that's a lot of sausage. Not only did the hog's weight set a record, but the size of his tusks—18 inches and 16 inches—also set a new Safari Club International North American free-range record.

Weird Encounters of the Georgia Kind

Alapaha, reveling in its fifteen minutes of fame, went hog wild and decided on a Hogzilla theme for their 2004 fall festival. There was a Hogzilla parade, a Hogzilla princess, Hogzilla T-shirts, and lots of little kids running around in pink pig costumes.

Visitors From Other Worlds

Atlanta / Marietta

September 1, 1952, was an active alien night in the Georgia skies. According to Project Blue Book, the U.S. government department in charge of debunking UFO sightings, Georgia citizens, including an Army Air Force B-25 gunner, an artillery officer, and thirty-five other just ordinary folks witnessed a light show of unprecedented proportions.

The sightings began in the skies over Atlanta at 9:43 p.m., when Mrs. William Davis and nine unnamed witnesses saw a bright light move up and down for a long period of time.

Next, at 10:30 p.m. in Marietta, an unidentified witness using binoculars saw two large objects shaped like a child's spinning top flying side by side. The tops displayed red, blue, and green lights and left a sparkling light trail for thirty minutes.

Coincidentally, at that same time in Marietta, an ex-artillery officer and twenty-four other witnesses saw a red, white, and blue-green object, which spun and shot off sparks for fifteen minutes.

At 10:50 in Marietta, an ex-Army Air Force gunner, who obviously wished to remain anonymous, saw two large, white disc-shaped objects with green vapor trails flying in formation. Merging, they then flew away.

Huh. Sounds like those aliens were putting on a fireworks display for us. However, Project Blue Book classified these sightings as "unknowns," something they are quite loathe to do.

BUENA VISTA

Is it possible that Georgia native Eddie Owens Martin received a visit from other-worldly creatures? Sometime in the late 1930s, while living in New York, Martin claimed that he was visited by a trio of exceedingly tall individuals who said they were from the future. Actually, they said, they were from the land of Pasaquan, a place where past, present, and future, and everything else, all come together. Martin, they further said, had been chosen by them to bring an understanding of the peace and beauty that the future holds for mankind. That is, if mankind would just listen.

Eddie Owens Martin was to become St. EOM (pronounced like a meditation mantra). The visitors told him how to communicate with and receive cosmic instruction from the "energies of the universe" on how to depict the futuristic world in art. He was to return to Georgia and "do something."

Well, St. EOM did, indeed, return to Georgia, where he spent thirty years setting the small town of Buena Vista on its ear. Take one look at St. EOM's artistic compound, whose futuristic buildings are enclosed by a wildly painted fence, and you could well believe that you're in another time and place—Africa maybe? Or Tibet? Perhaps the Incan Empire.

Before he died in 1986, St. EOM imbued the compound with a flamboyant energy, decked out in tribal garb, complete with feathered and beaded headdresses. Even today, visitors say the place emits a noticeable energy.

Call ahead at (229) 649-9444 if you plan to visit because like everything else here, the hours are not "regular" either.

Located on County Road 78 just outside of Buena Vista.

CONYERS

For many years now the Virgin Mary and son Jesus have been making regular visits to the small town of Conyers, and their favorite place to stay is at the rural home of housewife and mother Nancy Fowler.

It all began in February 1987, when Jesus appeared to Fowler, who was in deep despair. Although Jesus didn't speak, His visit changed her life. Then, on October 13, 1990, Fowler says she was visited by the Virgin Mary, who declared that she would be visiting with a message on the thirteenth of every month.

Obviously having kept up with the information age, Mary requested that Fowler photograph the Virgin Mary statue Fowler kept in her bedroom. She was to add the caption "Our Loving Mother" to the front of the photograph and on the back she should put the Angel's Prayer of Fatima "Oh, Most Holy Trinity," followed by "Let this prayer be echoed all over the world," and "Conyers, Georgia."

"Let the card be distributed far and wide," the Virgin decreed, "and many healings will occur." Fowler, said the Virgin, was the instrument chosen by God to give the world her image, and she should not delay in distributing this holy card.

Fowler did indeed distribute the card, and as the word got around that the Virgin would be making an appearance on the thirteenth of each month, thousands came for solace and healing. Then, after eight years, Fowler announced that the Virgin had informed her that October 13, 1998, would be her last appearance.

On that date, more than 100,000 believers from all over the world flocked to Conyers. Fowler appeared to the patiently waiting crowd and delivered the Virgin's final words: "My crowning words are to be holy, to be witnesses, and to walk in my faith. I love you all, my dear children." Many dropped to their knees and prayed for miracles. Others just prayed to find their cars.

The Virgin has not visited Fowler since that date, but thousands still make the pilgrimage to Conyers every year for the anniversary of the Virgin's last sighting. A church has been erected at Fowler's farm and the Our Loving Mother Shrine is maintained here on White Road.

EATONTON

The aliens have landed! Four hundred of 'em! And they're living in doublewides in Eatonton! But don't panic! They'll be leaving any day now on a spaceship bound for their home planet of Rizq.

The United Nuwaubian Nation of Moors, a fraternal society (read: religious cult), landed in Georgia in 1993 by way of Brooklyn (considered another planet by most Southerners!), when their leader, Dwight York, aka Dr. Michael York, aka

Weird Encounters of the Georgia Kind

Malachi York, aka Chief Black Eagle, bought a 476-acre game ranch in Eatonton. The group claims to be a part of the Yamassee Native-American tribe of Georgia and descendants of Egyptians who migrated from the Nile Valley to the Georgia countryside before continental drift separated the continents. Hey, it's their story and they're sticking to it.

But that's not the Strangest But Truest part of the story. York claims he's an alien from the planet Rizq in Illyuwn, the nineteenth galaxy. He assures his followers that a spaceship from Rizq will be arriving soon to take 144,000 lucky Nuwaubians home for rebirth.

Wonder how he explained the fact that the Rizqans missed his first deadline? Yep, May 5, 2003, came and went with nary a UFO in sight. Engine trouble, perhaps?

Anyway, those tardy aliens need to put the pedal to the metal and hurry up. In 2004, York was sentenced to 135 years in prison for molesting fourteen of his follower's children. How much is that in Rizq years, do ya think?

FRANKLIN

The little town of Franklin has seen its share of alien craft, too. Take, for example, July 5, 1996.

It was a peaceful, summer day, and three people fishing on the Chattahoochee River were drowsing over their fishing rods when an egg-shaped object, the size of a Volkswagen beetle, suddenly appeared! Buzzing over a nearby bridge, it dropped to hover about fifty feet above the water. It made no noise and did not disturb the water's surface.

Slowly, it turned to a horizontal position and began moving off at a ten mph clip. Clearing a kudzu patch and a pecan tree, it hovered briefly above some workmen (who never saw it), then moved on. It continued on to the town of Franklin, where it was sighted above the baseball field, and on out of town. It then suddenly turned back and flew back over Franklin, then disappeared out of sight.

Think maybe this was the Nuwaubian's limo, a few years early and a few miles off course? Really, it's so hard to calculate arrival times when you're dealing with all those light years.

LaGrange

LaGrange is a hotbed, we tell you! A hotbed of UFO activity! In fact, many go so far as to say that LaGrange is the UFO Capital of the Nation, although citizen Jack Thompson says he wouldn't go quite that far. Thompson is a local UFO investigator and state director of MUFON (Mutual UFO Network). He cites Gulf Breeze, Florida, and Pine Bush, New York, as two cities that are at least as UFO-active as LaGrange.

Thompson, who is also a local insurance agent, became interested in UFOs in 1994, when he and his family sighted a bright stream of lights, resembling Christmas tree lights, hovering one hundred feet above the ground near his home. The lights of red, blue, green, and white were circling an object that seemed to be spinning.

Grabbing his trusty video camera, Thompson was able to get about a minute of tape on the UFO before the battery died. After viewing the tape, a MUFON photo analyst declared the UFO sighting genuine, so it must be so.

That sighting was just one of many reported in the little town. Thompson says the first documented UFO sighting in LaGrange occurred in 1938, when a man reported seeing a UFO making erratic maneuvers and flying "faster than anything he had ever seen."

The year 1998 was especially active with a full-fledged UFO "flap" that began on January 8. At around 7:30 p.m. that evening, a couple driving down North Greenwood Street in LaGrange reported an intense beam of light coming from the clouds and down to the ground.

Incredibly, there were at least two more sightings in the following weeks that included reports of "a shiny dot zipping across the sky," and "a large white disc." What the aliens find so attractive about LaGrange is not known. Good schools, maybe? Perhaps they, like the town's fathers, believe it to be America's Greatest Little City.

LAVONIA

On June 29, 1964, businessman Beauford E. Parham (how's that for a grand old Southern name?) had a really close encounter of the Georgia kind. He was driving home late that evening when he saw a bright light in the sky coming toward him. It was a top-shaped object, spinning and hissing "like a million snakes," said Parham.

Amber in color, it was six to eight feet tall. There was a spire protruding from the top, and along the bottom were portholes through which flames were visible. It disappeared, then quickly returned and hovered in front of the headlights for about a mile, as Parham, in a trance-like state, sped down the country road at sixty-five mph.

The UFO moved up and over the car, leaving the strong odor of embalming fluid (Yikes!) and a gaseous vapor. Parham's encounter wasn't over, though. The ship returned, again flying directly in front of the headlights. Suddenly, the car began to sputter and Parham pulled to a stop, at which point the UFO did a crazy spin and took off.

Feeling a burning sensation on his arms, Parham drove to a nearby air base and reported his UFO to FAA officials, who detected radioactivity on the car, but made no formal report. Parham said that his arms continued to burn even after he washed them, and that there was an oily substance on the car that persisted through several washings. He also reported that the paint on the hood bubbled and the radiator and hoses deteriorated soon after the encounter.

LEARY

Georgia's most famous citizen is a believer. Back in 1969, then Governor Jimmy Carter looked up into the heavens and said, "What the heck is that?"

Carter believes it was a UFO. Others aren't so sure, citing that old North Star defense that non-believers are so fond of. But Carter stuck to his guns. During his 1976 Presidential campaign, he told a group of reporters about the sighting. It seems that he and about twelve of the Leary Georgia Lions Club members were standing outside waiting for the 7:30 p.m. meeting to begin. It was shortly after dark on a clear October evening. Looking up, someone noticed a very large light—about the size of the moon—moving toward them. This unidentified light was very bright and it changed colors. It came closer, moved away, came closer, and moved away, then disappeared.

"It was the darndest thing I've ever seen," Carter told the reporters. And he promised that, if elected, he would make every piece of the country's information on UFO sightings available to the public and scientists.

Jimmy Carter is not the only U.S. president to have sighted a UFO prior to serving in the White House. He shares this dubious distinction with Ronald Reagan, who reportedly witnessed two sightings before coming to live on Pennsylvania Avenue.

Eat, Drink, and Be Merry!

Eating Out

Eating out in Strange But True Georgia is more than a meal—it's an experience. There are restaurants and bars galore along the back roads trail, some historic, some haunted, some just plain fun.

AGAVE • ATLANTA
OK. This is our kinda place. Sure, the food's good, but, hey, check out that tequila bar! In addition to southwestern fare, Agave offers thirty-five different kinds of tequila. For all you tequila

Agave is famous for its wide selection of tequila.
Courtesy of Agave

connoisseurs out there, the selection includes Caba Wabo Anejo, Centenario Resposado, Herradura Seleccion Suprema (at a suprema $35 a pop), and Patron Platinum. Wooo Hooo! Let's parrrtay! Forget shooting it, though. These here are sipping tequilas. Show a little class, would ya?

   Located at 242 Boulevard Southeast.

Eat, Drink, and Be Merry!

THE BILLIARD ACADEMY • THOMASVILLE

On the hunt for a good old Georgia dawg—hot dawg, that is? Try the dogs at The Billiard Academy. They're so good that folks from as far away as Tallahassee drive all the way to Thomasville for one.

It's owner Joe Kirkland's tangy chili sauce that makes these pups so popular. And as an added bonus, after you've sated your appetite, you can enjoy a quick game of billiards. Food and entertainment. What more can you ask for?

The Billiard Academy is known far and wide for its chili dogs and its pool tables.
Courtesy of Downtown Thomasville Main Street

Located at 121 South Broad Street.

DINGLEWOOD PHARMACY • COLUMBUS

Next time you're in this fair city, be sure to stop by the lunch counter at Dinglewood Pharmacy for one of Lieutenant (You don't have to salute. That's his name.) Stevens's Scrambled Dogs. This culinary concoction is a diet staple in Columbus, having been around since the 1930s, when Dinglewood owner Henry "Sport" Brown first invented it. Stevens took over after Brown passed on in the 1950s, tweaking the recipe and making it his own.

So what is a Scrambled Dog? Relax, it's not a pooch that crossed the road too slow. To make a Scrambled Dog, you take two split hot dogs and a bun and place them in a banana-split dish. Pile on dill pickles, relish, mustard, and cheese. Cover the entire mess with Stevens's spicy, meaty, secret-recipe chili, crumble on a few oyster crackers, and voilà! A Scrambled Dog.

Stevens serves hundreds of his dogs every day at Dinglewood's lunch counter, which seats fifty-eight at a time. Patrons from three decades bring their children and grandchildren for initiation into this Columbus rite of passage.

Located at 1939 Wynnton Road.

FINCHER'S BBQ • MACON

Fincher's BBQ is probably the only restaurant in the world that can say its food is out of this world. At least it's been out of this world. Seems that when astronaut Manley "Sonny" Carter, a good ol' Macon boy, was selected for a mission on the space shuttle Discovery in 1989, he had to have his 'cue with him. He had a bunch of Fincher's freeze dried and hermetically sealed, so he could enjoy it as he circled the globe (seventy-nine times).

First opened in 1935, Fincher's serves up ribs, chicken, sandwiches, and reportedly some of the best Brunswick stew ever made. There's indoor seating and take out, but most folks take advantage of the 1950s style drive-in, where car hops take and bring your order.

Located at 3947 Houston Avenue.

4-WAY LUNCH • CARTERSVILLE

No, you can't have it your way at 4-Way Lunch. You get it their way or no way. Just read the sign: "This isn't Burger King. You don't get it your way; you get it our way, or you don't get the damn thing." Hmmmph.

Control issues aside, their way must be pretty good, 'coz when the place burned down a few years ago and the owner had no insurance and no way to rebuild, the whole town pitched in and rebuilt the little diner.

So, come in and enjoy their country diner eating. Just remember to shut up and eat.

Located at the corner of Main and Gilmer Streets.

THE LADY AND SONS • SAVANNAH

We like that Paula Deen. No, not because she has her own cooking show on the Food Network. And not because she has authored best-selling cookbooks. We like Paula because she is a good ol' Southern girl who grew up knowing what every Southerner knows: Southern food is comfort food.

Says Paula, "Southern cooking comes from within, and it's how we show our love...If your Southern food is authentic. It's not pretentious. It doesn't require a sophisticated palette [sic or maybe not. She may well have meant that Southern taste buds are a place to mix up colorful flavors. Makes perfect sense to us.]. The ingredients are distinctly Southern, and it's all home grown. The dishes don't require split-second timing, and they don't fall!"

The Lady and Sons Restaurant, the restaurant Paula owns with her two exceedingly handsome sons, carries through with

Paula's philosophies on Southern cooking. The menu includes such favorites as fried green tomatoes, chicken pot pie, meat loaf sandwich, and that true Southern favorite, the Southern

The Lady and Sons serves fine Southern cuisine under the ownership of Paula Deen.
Courtesy of Lady and Sons

buffet packed with all the goodies from your childhood: fried chicken, collard greens, mashed taters, and mac and cheese. All served with a big ol' glass of sweet tea and some cheese grits and hoecakes (that's cornbread cooked on a griddle pancake-style, for y'all Yankees).

OK, so there are some fancy things thrown in, too, such as crab stuffed Portobello mushrooms, crab cakes, calamari (that's squid to y'all who didn't grow up on the coast), and fried lobster. Umm umm. It's still good eatin'!

Located at 102 West Congress Street.

Nu-Way Weiner • Macon

Not long after James Mallis opened the Nu-way Weiner stand in 1916, his private-label franks smothered in all the fixin's and topped with his secret chili and a smattering of bar-b-cue sauce became an obsession with locals. And that obsession quickly spread.

Opened in 1916, Nu-Way Weiners still operates in its original thirty-nine seat building.
Courtesy of Nu-Way Weiners

The dawgs, which are still served from the original store with its neon sign and thirty-nine seats, have been recognized by such prestigious publications as *Gourmet*, *Southern Living*, and *Money* as some of the best dawgs in the country.

Located at 428 Cotton Avenue.

POOLE'S BAR-B-Q RESTAURANT • EAST ELLIJAY

Remember that Pig Hill of Fame we told you about? It's adjacent to Poole's Bar-B-Q Restaurant, considered by many North Georgia folks as the best in the country. That may be true, but one thing's for sure. You'll never find a place that's more pig-oriented.

The restaurant began as a roadside bar-b-q shack with no indoor seating in 1989. Word got around about the good food, and lo and behold, one cold February day, then Presidential candidate Pat Buchanan dropped in with a few friends—including five hundred members of the media. And, Wham! Bam! Poole's Bar-B-Q was the talk of the nation.

Not one to miss a marketing opportunity, owner Colonel (so designated by a governor of Kentucky) Oscar Poole took advantage of the sudden popularity to expand his operation and imbue it with his own brand of campy tackiness.

The shack is now a modern cabin-style restaurant named the Taj-Ma-Hog. There's seating—pine booths and a hodgepodge of mismatched chairs. And pigs, pigs, everywhere are pigs. Here a ceramic pig. There a stuffed pig. Everywhere a pig, pig.

Adjoining the Taj-Ma-Hog is the Hog-Rock Cafe, where Poole entertains guests with his "piano wizardry." Ear plugs might be advisable. In addition, there's the Pig-Moby-il, a 1976 Volare that has a few additions, such as pig ears and a snout. It oinks and snorts as it travels down the highways and byways of Strange But True Georgia.

Poole's marketing savvy draws in people from around the world, including state senators and governors, Olympic athletes, and a Miss America or two. You're like as not to find Porsches and Mercedes parked next to that old Pig-Moby-il.

So, enjoy the food. Get your name painted on a plywood pig, and don't forget to pick up a few bottles of the Colonel's original sauce for sale inside! But don't come on a Monday or a Tuesday. That's the pigs' days off.

Located at 164 Craig Street.

THE SWALLOW AT THE HOLLOW • ROSWELL

The Swallow at the Hollow ain't yore typical barbecue joint. Yes, it is just a shack—rustic inside and out. Yes, you're greeted at the door with "Hi, Y'all." And yes, the 'cue is good,

Eat, Drink, and Be Merry!

including all the favorites, ribs, sandwiches, and traditional sides.

BUT! There's a highbrow back 'ere in the kitchen som'eres. In addition to the traditional 'cue joint fare, The Swallow offers a couple of frou-frou dishes your MeeMaw never heard of.

The Swallow at the Hollow is a favorite among the locals.
Photo by Scott Housley

You'll find marinated BBQ pork pizza and pit cooked Portobello mushrooms with smoked gouda cheese and fried green tomatoes (they say tomato, we say maters). Ain't sayin' they ain't good. They jes different that's all.

On Friday and Saturday nights, The Swallow offers a variety of live music. Come early, because this place is popular with the locals.

Located at 1072 Green Street.

THE TOUCAN CAFÉ • SAVANNAH
Wishing you could've gone a little farther south for your vacation? Well, stop in at The Toucan Café, a little touch of the Caribbean in Jawjah. Be sure to wear your sunglasses—inside. This place is really bright, painted in vibrant hues of

lime green, shocking pink, bright yellow, and deep purple. Even the bar is a vivid limey green! All tablecloths and furniture have matching colors.

The food is an eclectic mix of Caribbean, Mediterranean, and down-home Southern fare. You'll find such choices as Jamaican jerk chicken, filet mignon with demi-glace, and Hellenic chicken (stuffed with spinach and feta cheese). Or you can go the meat and whipped potatoes route.

There may be a wait, but owners Steve and Nancy Magulias say no one minds. They just take advantage of the festive, whimsical atmosphere.

Located at 531 Stephenson Avenue.

UNCLE BUBBA'S OYSTER HOUSE • SAVANNAH

Paula Deen's brother, Bubba (of course!), can cook, too, it seems. He recently opened Uncle Bubba's Oyster House on Whitmarsh Island. Its claim to fame is the chargrilled oysters, cooked right on the dining room floor over an open flame, and good ol' fresh Southern seafood. There's live music on Thursday, Friday, and Saturday nights.

Uncle Bubba's Oyster House is famous for its chargrilled oysters.
Photo by Sunny Lee

Located at 104 Bryan Woods Road.

Eat, Drink, and Be Merry!

THE VARSITY • ATLANTA/ ATHENS

The World's Largest Drive-In! The Varsity is a Georgia landmark. It was opened in 1928 by Frank Gordy, a Georgia native who, when he flunked out of Georgia Tech in 1925, told a classmate that he'd be worth $20,000 (hey, it was a lot of money back then!) by the time his class graduated.

He used a $2,000 nest egg and opened a small drive-in restaurant at the crossroads of Luckie Street and North Avenue. Calling it the Yellow Jacket (Georgia Tech's football team), he sold hot dogs and bottled Coke to Georgia Tech students. The restaurant was a big hit, and in no time, Gordy was searching for a larger place. He'd also doubled that prediction to his friend—by the time his old class graduated, he was worth $40,000.

Moving the restaurant to a larger location on North Avenue, with a larger menu, he changed

The Varsity now has seven locations and boasts of being the World's Largest Drive-In.
Courtesy of The Varsity

the name to The Varsity to accommodate his plans to open restaurants in other Georgia college towns.

Gordy had big ideas to bring in the customers. He started the first ever curb service in Georgia. Customers would pull up to the curb next to the restaurant and pay a young man to run inside and get their order. It was a popular service, but one that spawned an unexpected problem: The enterprising owner of the diner across the street started sending out a young man to take orders, cutting into The Varsity's business. Gordy responded by buying an adjoining parking lot for his customers to park. Problem solved. His curb service was so popular, that within a few years, that one young man was one of one hundred Varsity car hops.

Gordy's innovations didn't stop there. These were the days before orange soda came in a bottle, so he traveled far and wide—all the way to Noow Yawk City—in search of the perfect recipe for this syrupy treat so he could make it himself. To keep up with the increasing demand for his dogs and fried pies, he designed a hot dog conveyor belt and a pie-making machine. He was the first to place TVs in a restaurant, and indeed, many Georgia citizens got their first glimpse of this newfangled machine at The Varsity. Finally, when the parking lot became too small for the growing crowds, he built a parking deck.

In 1932, Gordy opened another Varsity at 101 College Avenue in Athens, a smaller version of the Atlanta store, complete with TV viewing rooms. In 1965 The Varsity Jr. was opened at 1085 Lindbergh Drive in Atlanta by Gordy's son, Frank Jr. With recent expansion, there are now four locations in Atlanta and locations in Gwinnet and Alpharetta.

The original location at 61 North Avenue in Atlanta is the largest and most popular. As The World's Largest Drive-In, it accommodates six hundred cars and more than eight hundred people at once. And on days of Georgia Tech football games, the restaurant boasts of serving as many as thirty thousand customers.

More than two miles of hot dogs, a ton of onion rings, twenty-five hundred pounds of potatoes, five thousand French fries, and five thousand fried pies are served daily, and the restaurant is the world's largest single restaurant outlet for Coca-Cola sales. Their food is made from scratch—including fresh cut fries and homemade chili.

Step in and you'll be greeted with the famous Varsity chant, which began when crowds packed in during the restaurant's early days: "What'll ya have ... What'll ya have ... Have your order in mind and your money in hand."

The World's Largest Kitchen is located in Milledgeville at the Center State Hospital, which is reported to be capable of preparing thirty thousand meals a day.

Miscellaneous Miscellany

More points of strangeness along the Strange But True Georgia trail.

It's The Law!

Better watch your step in our Strange But True Georgia. You never know when the long arm of the law may reach out and nab you for breaking some of these strange but true laws!

1. It's illegal to use profanity in front of a dead body lying in a funeral home or in a coroner's office. Show a little respect.

2. It's illegal to carry an ice cream cone in your pocket on Sunday. It's OK any other day, but things could get a bit sticky.

3. Simple battery is permitted if provoked by fighting words. Ooo, you've said it now. Put up yur dukes! Them's fightin' words!

4. In Atlanta it's against the law to tie a giraffe to a telephone pole or street lamp. Bet there's a really tall tale behind this law.

5. In Gainesville, chicken must be eaten with the hands. Hmmm…we didn't know chickens had hands.

6. It's illegal for chickens to cross the road in Quitman. But, officer. It had to get to the other side!

7. Donkeys are not to be kept in the bathtub. Just bathe them and get them out.

8. In Marietta, it's illegal to spit from a car or a bus, but you can spit from a truck. Hey, didn't yore mama teach you better?

9. In Acworth, all citizens must own a rake. Nothing says you have to use it though.

10. All sex toys are banned in the state of Georgia. Ooo La La!

11. Erotic dancing is prohibited on Sundays in Roswell. Now, stop that Ethel. It's Sunday, you know.

12. Also in Roswell, the flooring of adult bookstores and video stores must be nonabsorbent and smooth textured. EWW! Don't even wanna think about it.

Strange Town Names

The laws in some of our Georgia towns aren't the only thing that's strange. How about some of the names of the towns and how they came to be?

BETWEEN • WALTON COUNTY

Yep. That's the name of the town. It was named by a former postmaster because it lies halfway between Monroe and Loganville.

CLIMAX • DECATUR COUNTY

Shame on you! So named because it's the highest point on the railroad between Savannah and the Chattahoochee River.

ENIGMA • BERRIEN COUNTY

It's a mystery to us.

HOPEULIKIT • BULLOCH COUNTY

This little town in Bulloch County was named for a honkytonk. Seems there was a famous dance hall nearby, and folks musta liked it so much they named the town for it.

SOCIAL CIRCLE • WALTON COUNTY

There's speculation that this town was named by the first group of settlers, who liked to pass around a jug of spirits every now and then. They considered themselves a social circle.

TALKING ROCK • PICKENS COUNTY

According to legend, this town is named for an unusual echo that was supposed to emanate from a nearby rock cliff.

THUNDERBOLT • CHATHAM COUNTY

Story is this small town is so named for a powerful bolt of lightning that created a freshwater spring on Wilmington bluff. Lightning musta struck twice, for this incident doesn't seem to be related to our previous story about Providence Spring.

WILLACOOCHEE • ATKINSON COUNTY

Willacoochee is thought to be an Indian name meaning "Home of the Wildcat."

Towns of Note

ABBEVILLE • WILCOX COUNTY

As you may have guessed by now, there's lots of pork in Georgia. Pigs on the hill. Hogzilla. No place is piggier than Abbeville, however. It's known as the Wild Hog Capital of Georgia. It's also known as the Camellia City of the South.

> Georgia's Cumberland Island is the largest undeveloped island on the Atlantic Coast. The ruins of the once magnificent Carnegie estate, Dungeness, are on the seashore here.

ADEL • COOK COUNTY

San Juan Capistrano has nothing on little Adel, Georgia. Just as the swallows return to San Juan Capistrano, so do the buzzards return to Adel. Yep, every December hundreds of the repulsive creatures flock to Reed Bingham State Park, where they frolic away the winter.

Their return is celebrated the first Saturday in December with a Buzzard Day Festival, when hundreds of humans flock to the park to gawk at the buzzards and participate in various festivities.

AMERICUS • SUMTER COUNTY

Americus, named for explorer Amerigo Vespucci, is a high-flying town. In 1923, a fledgling pilot named Charles Lindbergh traveled to Americus's Souther Field to purchase his first airplane, a surplus

World War I "Jenny." Lindbergh flew his first solo over southwest Georgia in his new plane. He must've enjoyed it. Four years later, he made history with his solo flight over the Atlantic.

Lindbergh attested to his Americus flight with a plaque at the former Souther Field, now the Americus airport. The plaque reads: "I had not soloed up to the time I bought my Jenny at Americus, Georgia."

Charles Lindbergh flew his first solo flight at Souther Field. Courtesy of www.jerrybattle.com

ATHENS • CLARKE COUNTY

Known as the "Classic City" for all its Greek Revival buildings, Athens is the county seat and is home to the University of Georgia. That's not all that makes this Georgia town notable. Believe it or not, Athens is a rockin' city. In music circles it's known as The Liverpool of the South for having birthed such bands as the B-52s and R.E.M., not to mention the Tone Tones and Widespread Panic.

Athens also is home to the University of Georgia, the country's first state-chartered university. The college was incorporated on January 27, 1785, making Athens the birthplace of America's public higher education system.

Because the university's first president was a Yale man, UGA has strong ties to that venerable institution. Many of the first campus buildings were designed from blueprints of Yale buildings, and UGA's football team was nicknamed the "Bulldogs"—after the Yale team.

The campus now encompasses 4,308 acres, divided into the North Campus, which holds the original historic buildings, and the South Campus, comprised of new additions.

Athens is full of Greek architecture, including this statue of Athena.
Courtesy of Jeff Montgomery, Athens-Clarke County Public Information Office

AUGUSTA • RICHMOND COUNTY

Woodrow Wilson, born in Virginia, came to Augusta in 1858, when his father accepted the position as pastor to Augusta's First Presbyterian Church. The thirteen years he spent here is more time than he spent anywhere else, which, of course, includes his eight years in the White House.

Wilson is quoted as saying that his earliest memory was in Augusta, when a family friend broke the news to his father that Lincoln had been elected and there was to be a war. Indeed, the young Wilson experienced the war first-hand as it was fought in Augusta.

Wilson's ties to Georgia remained strong throughout his life. He briefly practiced law in Atlanta, married a minister's daughter from Rome, and witnessed the birth of his first daughter in a Gainesville hotel.

The Augusta boyhood home was recently opened as a museum at 419 Seventh Street.

COLUMBUS • MUSCOGEE COUNTY
Columbus is home to Fort Benning, the largest infantry camp in the world.

FLOWERY BRANCH • HALL COUNTY
This town with the pretty name is reputed to be the home of the Porter House steak. In the early 1900s, it seems that the Porter family owned a restaurant here, and their method of cooking a steak was so popular with traveling salesmen and trainmen that soon the "Porter House" steak appeared on menus everywhere.

HARLEM • COLUMBIA COUNTY
Yep, there's a Harlem, Georgia. Located in the southern part of the state, this little town is the birthplace of Oliver Hardy, the rotund half of the comedy team Laurel and Hardy.

HELEN • WHITE COUNTY
Well, here's something strange but true. A little bit of Bavaria in the Deep South. Helen got its start in the late 1800s as an unnamed shanty town, founded by miners caught up in the Great Georgia Gold Rush. When the gold ran out, so did the settlers.

Miscellaneous Miscellany

Next came the Great Timber Rush. Loggers took one look at the miles and miles of virgin timber in the surrounding valley and saw lots of green—money, that is. Staking their claim, the Matthews Lumber Company

Helen, Georgia, offers a taste of Bavaria in the Deep South.
Photo by Zeny Williams

built a large sawmill and founded a new town, named Helen for the daughter of a Matthews Company manager.

Years of cutting the lumber without replanting stripped the land, and the loggers decided to move on. The sawmill closed in 1931, and Helen struggled for a new identity.

The federal government had purchased the devastated land to establish the Georgia National Forest, now called the Chattahoochee National Forest. The land was replanted, and through the growth years, Helen tried to establish itself as a tourism town—without much success. By the 1960s, the town was just a collection of shabby buildings until three Helen citizens got together with a plan. Aware of the success that Hamilton, Georgia, enjoyed simply by repainting its storefronts, the men hired John Kollack, a local artist, to repaint Helen.

Kollack, an ex-military man who had spent several years in Germany, had grander ideas. How about Bavaria, Georgia-style?

Huh. Who knew that an Alpine village was just what Georgia tourists were hankerin' for? Beer gardens, wienerschnitzel, cuckoo clocks, and, oh! How about that funky serenade—with an accordion, no less, played by guys in lederhosen. Who knew?

Shop 'til you drop in the charming little stores, where you'll find all sorts of imported gee gaws. Visit during Oktoberfest to get the full Bavarian feel. There's lots of beer and plenty of fun and dancing to happy oom-pah bands. An added bonus is the beauty of the Blue Ridge Mountains in full fall colors.

KNOXVILLE • CRAWFORD COUNTY

The name of this town might bring Tennessee to mind, but Texas is the state with which this Georgia town has strong ties. It seems that back in 1835, Texas sent out a plea for help in gaining its independence from Mexico. With true Southern spirit, Georgia raised a battalion to send to Texas.

To assist them, local teenager Joanna Troutman designed and sewed a flag featuring a blue star with five points. The Georgia battalion took it with them when they joined Colonel James Fanin in south Texas. When Fanin learned that Texas had won its independence on March 2, 1836, he raised the torn flag as the national flag, the first Lone Star flag to fly over a free Texas.

MADISON • MORGAN COUNTY

Since the 1800s, Madison has sported the reputation as a great place to live. An 1845 guide to Georgia touted it as "the most aristocratic and cultured town on the stagecoach route from Charleston to New Orleans."

Much more recently—in 2000—Madison was named "The

Best Small Town in America" by *Travel Holiday* magazine, which cited the town's low crime rate, good schools, and cultural attractions as the reasons for the award.

Madison bills itself as "the town Sherman refused to burn." Indeed, it was spared destruction during Sherman's March to the Sea, although those greedy Yankees did loot the place. Took off with anything that wasn't nailed down.

With a population of just five thousand, Madison is blessed with Southern charm. Walking the streets of its historic district, built around the Post Office Square, takes you back to a time of gentility and tranquility.

That's not to say that Madison is hopelessly behind the times. Oh, contraire! You'll find fine dining and accommodations, art galleries, and world class golf and tennis resorts. Just the right blend of the old and the new.

MORELAND • COWETA COUNTY

"American by birth. Southern by the grace of God" was the motto of Georgia's favorite son, Lewis Grizzard. Often called "this generation's Mark Twain," Grizzard grew up in Moreland and frequently poked affectionate fun at his small hometown.

Grizzard's column and books extolled the Southern way of living and introduced the Southern Redneck to the world. Throughout the 1980s and early 1990s, he became a celebrity, showing off his storytelling and comedic skills on such shows as the *Tonight Show starring Johnny Carson*, *Larry King Live*, and *Tomorrow*.

A frequent subject in Grizzard's writing was the trials he faced with his personal health. Because of a congenital heart defect, he suffered a series of near-death experiences and endured three open heart surgeries. He never quite recovered from his last surgeries, and on March 20, 1994, he suffered a fatal heart attack while playing golf in Orlando, Florida.

Fans can visit his grave site at the Moreland Cemetery in Moreland. If you really want to pay tribute, however, make a pilgrimage to the 50-yard line at the University of Georgia's Sanford Stadium. Seems Grizzard, an alumnus of UGA, was a rabid Dogs fan. It was his last wish to be cremated and have his ashes spread on the stadium's 50-yard line. His family halfway honored that wish, spreading half his ashes there and interring the rest in the Moreland Cemetery.

PERRY • HOUSTON COUNTY

Perry is slap dab in the middle of it all. It's known as the Crossroads of Georgia, because it's the town closest to the center of the state.

THOMASVILLE • THOMAS COUNTY

The entire world, including most of Georgia, believes that the

A look at downtown Perry shows beautiful streets in the Crossroads of Georgia.
Courtesy of the Perry Area Convention and Visitors Bureau

epic movie *Gone With the Wind* premiered at Loew's Grand Theater in Atlanta. The entire world, including most of Georgia, is wrong. The movie was shown for the first time in the private theater of Mel Hanna Jr., a wealthy industrialist who owned a large plantation in Thomasville.

Seems that Hanna was good friends with John "Jock" Whitney, the filthy rich New Yorker who had helped finance production of the movie. Once the movie was finished, producers approached Whitney with their hands out once more—hoping for some cashola to put toward marketing. Before he shelled out any more of his hard-earned millions, however, Whitney insisted on seeing what he was getting. Desperate, the movie's producers sent a finished reel to Hanna's plantation, and it was shown to Hanna, Whitney, and forty of their closest friends.

We're assuming Whitney was pleased, for he forked over the money and the rest is history.

The Cherokee Rose is the official state flower, the live oak tree is the official state tree, and the official state bird is the brown thrasher.

Funny Happenings Here

Bobbin' for pig's feet, brewin' up some good ol' corn liquor, rollin' in grits....There's just no end to the funny goings on in Strange But True Georgia.

ALL-AMERICAN HAPPY DAZE • DAWSONVILLE

Miss the good ol' days? Well, come on down to the Amicalola Falls State Park near Dawsonville and take a step back to a simpler time. Here you can celebrate Independence Day with nostalgic activities such as Hula Hoop contests, hayrides, pie-eating contests, and a greased pole climb. After all that, pop over to the park's restaurant, magically transformed into the 1950s-style Amicalola Diner, for a quick burger. Who knows? Maybe even the Fonz'll drop in. Heeeyyy.

ATLANTA CELTIC FESTIVAL • ATLANTA

Here's a bit of Georgia history you may be unaware of: Georgia was founded by settlers from Ireland, Scotland, and Wales who came to protect the fledgling colony from the evil Spaniards. These emigrants established a rich cultural heritage, from which many Southern traditions are derived. Country fiddling, bluegrass music, folksongs, tap dancing, and tall-tale telling all originate from this history.

That's why in 2005 Georgia Governor Sonny Perdue officially proclaimed May 15-21 as Celtic Heritage Week. The action was taken to encourage Georgia citizens to explore their

Celtic roots and learn more about the culture that so influenced the state's history.

The week of ceremonies and programs culminates with the Atlanta Celtic Festival, a weekend of song, dance, and "criac." (As we understand it, criac means anything that makes you immensely happy!)

You'll hear music from bands like Keltic Kudzu, Mickle-A-Do, Shanveen, and Emerald Rose. The music ain't your down home country pickin', but no doubt, you find similarities, since Celtic music gave birth to both country fiddling and bluegrass music.

The festival also has Irish and Scottish dancing—you know, where the feet dance a jig, but the rest of the body never moves—exhibitions of Celtic antiquities, and workshops on all things Celtic.

There's lots of criac going on, so come on, Paw, grab yore kilt and let's hit the high road!

Blessing of the Fleet • Brunswick / Darien

The Blessing of the Fleet is a beautiful, centuries-old tradition that's believed to ensure a safe and bountiful season for fishermen. Although it originated in southern Europe, the tradition has been adopted by many American coastal towns, including the Georgia towns of Brunswick and Darien.

Brunswick adopted the tradition more than sixty years ago, when the town's Portuguese immigrants introduced it to their new community. Closely tied to the local Catholic church, St. Francis Xavier, the event is held on Mother's Day to honor both Our Lady of Fatima, the patron saint of Portugal, and mothers of the parish.

The Blessing of the Fleet begins with a morning mass and a ceremonial crowning of the Our Lady of Fatima statue. After the crowning, a parade ensues. An honor guard of the Knights of Columbus leads the parishioners around Hanover Square, while a contingent of eight men carry the crowned statue. The base of the statue is decorated with red and white flowers. Red symbolizes living mothers and white symbolizes those who have passed. An anchor made of red and white flowers is also placed on the statue's base.

After a turn or two around the square, the parade proceeds to the waterfront, where shrimp trawlers—garishly decorated with streamers, signs, and American flags—putter around the harbor. As family and friends look on from the pier, the priest from St. Francis Xavier steps onto a boat, sprinkles holy water, and blesses each passing boat.

Then, the boats move on to St. Simon's Sound, where the priest drops the flower anchor overboard in memory of fishermen who've lost their lives on the sea.

Darien has been celebrating the Blessing of the Fleet only since 1970, but the tradition is a bigger deal in this small coastal town. Since it's scheduled to coincide with a falling tide (a rising tide would push the boats into the bridge), the date of the event varies. It's held on the Darien River on a Sunday afternoon in the spring.

The festivities begin early in the week with an evening prayer service, a fisherman's fish fry, and a parade through the streets. Boat owners spend weeks cleaning, painting, and decorating their boats to compete for the trophies and prizes given away at the end of the blessing. For the blessing ceremony, local clerics of various denominations stand on the bridge above the river and bless each boat as it passes by.

BUGGY DAYS • BARNESVILLE

Naw. We're not celebrating insects. We're celebrating buggies—you know, wagons, carts…that kinda thing. Seems that back in the 1800s, when the horse and buggy was still the main mode of travel, Barnesville was known as the Buggy Capital of the South, thanks to the five buggy manufacturing companies located here.

Held on the third full weekend in September, Buggy Days has been named a Top 20 Event by the Southeast Tourism Society five years out of eight. The weekend is chock full of things to do. Try out your legs in the Buggython Road Race, where you can run or walk a 10K or 5K. There's also a one-mile Fun Walk and a Run and See Georgia Grand Prix Race. Kids will enjoy the Old Fashioned Games, where they compete to catch a prize pig, and the Bill Gill Express for Kids, where they can take a special train ride. They'll also love the "exhilarating adventure" of the Buggy Blast Fun Park, which features pony rides, a rock climbing wall, and a spider jump (OK, that's a little buggy). Don't miss the Annual Buggy Days Parade, the arts and crafts festival, and the fireworks display.

CHERRY BLOSSOM FESTIVAL • CONYERS

Who knew a Japanese tree could engender such devotion in the South? In Conyers, the first cherry trees were donated by Hideo Ogino, a former president of the Maxwell Corporation of America. In 1982, a festival was organized to nurture the friendship and exchange of Japanese culture. That first festival featured Japanese cooking classes, origami exhibits, Kabuki Theater, and karate demonstrations. Not your typical down-South festival, huh?

It's really grown from there, with the basic tenet the same—to encourage cultural friendship and understanding. The festival, timed to coincide with the blooming of the cherry trees, is now a month-long event, culminating in a weekend of festivities. There's music—three stages with continuous live entertainment—dancing, games, multi-cultural activities, an international food court, and crafts.

COWBOYS AND INDIANS DAYS • CARTERSVILLE

So what if this is the deep South? We can play cowboys and Indians, too. And forget about that PC stuff. Cowboys and Native Americans Day just ain't got the same ring to it.

This month-long celebration honors Georgia's Native American culture and spotlights Cartersville's Booth Western Museum, an eighty thousand square foot museum dedicated to Western Art.

Throughout the month of October, visitors can enjoy exhibits of fine arts and crafts, including paintings, jewelry, basketry, quilting, weaving, pottery, and photography. Weekends are especially lively, with live music, plenty of food, and fun signature events, such as Cookin' On The Range and the Etowah Valley Indian Festival.

So, saddle up, podner, and come on down.

Funny Happenings Here

DUKES OF HAZZARD FAN CLUB CONVENTION • COVINGTON

Yee Haw! Don't you just miss them good ol' boys Bo and Luke? And what about Daisy Duke struttin' around in those itty bitty shorts that are now named for her? Miss her, too? Well, then, jump in that old jalopy of yorn and head out for Covington. You just can't miss the *Dukes of Hazzard* Fan Club convention, held in Covington in July. You'll get a gander at the Dukes' personal collections and rare memorabilia, and may even catch sight of an original cast member or two. Yee Haw!

EUHARLEE COVERED BRIDGE FESTIVAL • EUHARLEE

They're dancing in the streets in Euharlee. You can dance, too. Come to the Euharlee Covered Bridge Festival and you can not only dance in the streets, but you can also witness a mock court, ogle fancy and antique cars, eat lots and lots of good food, and purchase fine arts and crafts. There'll be live music and plenty of activities for the kiddies.

Don't miss it! Held in September.

EUHARLEE POW WOW • EUHARLEE

Wow! It's an authentic Native American Pow Wow! Euharlee has a rich Native American history. The town's name is derived from the Native American "Eufaula," which means "she laughs as she runs." So what better place to convene a Pow Wow?

Held in October, the Pow Wow features intertribal dancing, Native American drums, storytelling, arts and crafts, and Native American food.

GEORGIA MOUNTAIN FAIR • HIAWASSEE

For twelve whole days in July, Hiawassee is filled with music, food, and fun. OK, so the kick-off Flower Show is a little sedate, but it really picks up after that. There are concerts every day with country music greats, such as Joe Diffie, The Bellamy Brothers, T.G. Shepard, and Ricky Van Shelton. There's down home country pickin' with Fiddlin' Howard Cunningham and the Georgia Mountain Fair Staff Band; gospel singing and bluegrass music; clog dancing; carnival rides; crafts and exhibits. And a bear show. Oh, my!

A woman demonstrates how to make lye soap at the Georgia Mountain Fair. Courtesy of Jim and Lisa Bryant/ Georgia Mountain Fair

You can also learn about the good old days, with the Old Ways Demonstrations, where the local folks show you how things used to be. They'll show you moonshine making (a useful skill, no doubt!), corn milling, cider squeezing, pork skin frying, blacksmithing, soap making, and quilting. Then you can tour the Pioneer Village to see how folks lived back in the day.

If you can't make it in July, don't despair. You can attend the Georgia Mountain Fall Festival in October and enjoy most of the same fun.

Funny Happenings Here

GREAT LOCOMOTIVE CHASE FESTIVAL • ADAIRSVILLE
The Great Locomotive Chase is celebrated annually in
Adairsville. This festival, held the first weekend in October,
features all manner of live music, from country to bluegrass to
gospel, with a little rock thrown in for good measure. There are
gun fight reenactments, heritage demonstrations, street dancing,
arts and crafts, carnival rides, fireworks, beauty pageants,
parades, and, of course, plenty of good ol' Southern cookin'.

INTERNATIONAL CHERRY BLOSSOM FESTIVAL • MACON
Macon, Georgia, has been named in the Congressional Record
as The Cherry Blossom Capital of the World, and with little
wonder. More than two hundred eighty-five thousand Yoshino
cherry trees line the streets, highways, and byways of this
quintessential Southern town.

And, as you may have guessed, there's a history behind them
thar trees. Seems that back in 1949, Macon realtor William
Fickling Sr. became enamored of the tree in his back yard that
bloomed so beautifully every spring. He had no idea what it was.
Neither did anyone else—not even Fickling's own gardener.

But then one day, on a visit to Washington D.C., Fickling
discovered a bunch of trees that looked just like the one in his
yard. He inquired and learned that the tree was a Yoshino
cherry tree, a species that was rare in the South. Not for long—
at least for Macon.

Fickling began growing the trees and freely sharing them
with his neighbors and the community. Soon Yoshino cherry
trees were blooming everywhere, but there were more to come.

In the 1970s, Macon citizen Carolyn Crayton asked Fickling to donate trees to be planted in her Wesleyan neighborhood. He agreed and before long there were trees in all neighborhoods.

In 1982, Crayton, who was executive director of the Keep Macon-Bibb Beautiful Commission, helped to establish a festival to showcase the cherry trees and honor Fickling for his contributions. Like Fickling's saplings, the festival has blossomed from a three-day party into a ten-day event that regularly garners international attention.

Macon's International Cherry Blossom Festival celebrates the beauty of flowering Yoshino cherry trees in the Cherry Blossom Capital of the World. Photo by Glenn Grossman

The International Cherry Blossom Festival features hundreds of activities spanning the ten days, including dances, street parties, concerts, parades, contests, a fashion show, an arts and crafts festival, a hot air balloon show, and fireworks. More than seven hundred thousand people attended the 2005 festival, which has been recognized as one of the top events in the U.S. and is listed as one of the top one hundred in North America.

And, just think. It all started with just one little cherry tree.

Funny Happenings Here

KINGSLAND CATFISH FESTIVAL • KINGSLAND

Every true Southerner knows the delight of catfish fried light, served with hushpuppies and a big ol' glass of tea so sweet it makes your teeth hurt. It's no wonder, then, that Georgians see fit to hold annual festivals in honor of this bewhiskered bottom feeder.

The Kingsland Catfish Festival, held on Labor Day weekend, is a weekend packed with food and fun. Events include free

Cecil the Catfish, the official mascot of the Kingsland Catfish Festival, is escorted by Kingsley the Lion during a parade.
Courtesy of Kingsland Convention & Visitors Bureau

concerts with well-known country music entertainers, baseball tournaments, a parade, a 5K run, a classic car and tractor exhibit, and a bicycle race. And if that's not enough, you'll also find arts and crafts, antiques and collectibles, children's rides, and food booths, which, of course, feature lots and lots of catfish.

The festival was named a 2004 Top 100 Events in North America by the American Bus Association and was twice named to the Southeast Tourism Society's Top 20 Events.

MOUNTAIN MOONSHINE FESTIVAL • DAWSONVILLE

"Look out, Paw! Revenooers are comin'!" OK. So, you won't hear that cry during this festival. See, the moonshinin' is legal

The Keep Macon-Bibb Beautiful Commission, started in 1974, was the model program for the first commission under the nation's Keep America Beautiful System.

here. And it's brewed for a good cause. All proceeds go to the StarBright Foundation, a group of local volunteers who raise money to bring Christmas to the less fortunate families in Dawson County.

The festival was the dream of Fred Goswick, a moonshiner from way back, who outran many a revenue agent during his whiskey-running days. Goswick, a folk artist and storyteller extraordinaire, held the first festival in the 1960s. He set up a couple of tables of his wood carvings, vegetables, and a small working still and told his moonshine-running tales to all who stopped by. News of the festival spread by word of mouth, and soon tourists began flocking to it. Last year, more than eighty thousand people attended.

One of the festival's main attractions is the race car show, where many racing stars come to display their rides. There are also antique cars—and drivers—on display. Many old timers come to reminisce about the good old days in Dawson County, where NASCAR got its start. They'll be glad to tell you of those days, when they outran the gov'ment at night and raced each other on weekends.

There are also cloggers and clowns and gospel singers. You can get an up close and personal view of a real Georgia whiskey still and then go pan for a little gold.

Despite its illicit theme, this festival is fun for the whole family.

On February 12, 2002, a resolution was passed that recognized Warwick, Georgia, as the Grits Capital of Georgia. A law was passed on April 20, 2002, that recognized grits as the official prepared food of the state of Georgia.

MULE DAY • CALVARY

Calvary is a really small town. Only about two hundred people call it home. But on the first Saturday in November, as many as ninety thousand herd into the hamlet to join in the annual Mule Day festivities. Now why anyone would want to celebrate an animal that epitomizes cussedness, we're not sure, but little Calvary does so with abandon. In fact, Mule Day is so popular that it has grown into Mule Days, with festivities beginning on Friday. And what a celebration it is!

There is, of course, live entertainment and plenty of food to be had. There are arts and crafts, a flea market, a petting zoo, and a parade. All the things you pretty much expect in a celebration such as this.

Ah, but then things get really different—and fun! First, there's the Mule Show, with prizes awarded in such categories as Best Jackass, Best Horse Mule, Best Riding Pleasure Mule, and Best Mare Mule. There are other mule activities, including Mule Barrel Racing, a Mule Log Pull, a driving contest (no, the mule's not driving—it's pulling a wagon), a plowing contest, and a hilarious best Mule Costume contest.

Then there are the human-type activities. Back in the day,

syrup making was big in Georgia, and mules were a big part of that production. You'll find demonstrations in cane grinding and syrup making. There's also a Sling Shot Turkey Shoot and a Panty Hose Race.

NATIONAL GRITS FESTIVAL • WARWICK

This may be a national festival, but we bet there ain't many Yankees making the trip down for the festivities. They don't know what they're missing! In addition to the usual festival-type activities, they have corn-shelling contest, a grits eating contest, and a Roll-in-the-Quaker-Instant-Grits Contest. In this uniquely Southern event, contestants leap into a trough filled with cooked grits. The contestant emerging from the trough with the most grits adhering to his body wins. Now that's entertainment!

Celebrated the second weekend in April.

REDNECK GAMES • EAST DUBLIN

Bobbin' fer pig's feet…the mud pit belly flop…the Butt Crack Competition…the Armpit Serenade….These are just a sampling of the grueling events competitors face in Georgia's Redneck Games. They began as a spoof of the 1996 Olympic Games, held in Atlanta, but in the ensuing years, they've grown into a phenomenon in their own right. Last year more than fifteen thousand attended to watch everything from the Lighting of the Ceremonial Grill to the awarding of Budweiser-can trophies. An international audience watched by way of MTV and BBC in London.

The Redneck Games, which are held in July, may not be as well-known as the Olympics, but the competitors still train religiously. They spend hours pumping out those twelve-ounce curls (Budweiser seems to be the equipment of choice) and packing in that good ol' Southern fried food to build the flabby abs needed for the mud pit belly flop.

Hey, we have the perfect slogan for the Redneck Games! Remember the famous last words of a redneck? "Hey, Bubba. Watch this!"

SWINE TIME • CLIMAX

Georgians sure do love pigs. They even have a festival honoring the little porkers. Held the first Saturday after Thanksgiving, the Swine Time Festival in Climax features such piggy events as a hog calling contest, pig racing, a best dressed pig contest, and a greased pig chase. It also has lots of live entertainment, carnival rides,

A production of *The Three Little Pigs* is one of the ways the pig is celebrated at the Swine Time Festival.
Courtesy of Climax Community Club

food (yes, you can sample chitlins), a parade, and arts and crafts.

VIDALIA ONION FESTIVAL • VIDALIA

No one knows why, but the onion seed that produces a hot onion elsewhere, produces an onion so sweet it can be eaten like an apple when grown in the soil around Vidalia. In the seventy years since this phenomenon was first discovered, the Vidalia onion has become quite famous and is sold around the world.

To celebrate the sweet little onion—and the economic boon it's brought to the state—the folks of Vidalia put on a festival. Held at harvest time, the festival features a vast array of events, including a Miss Vidalia Onion Beauty Pageant, a softball tournament, Vidalia onion cooking contests, a carnival, a rodeo, and an air show featuring the Blue Angels Navy Flight Demonstration Squadron.

Georgia really takes its Vidalia onions seriously. In 1986, the legislature trademarked them, an act which requires that Vidalia onion producers and packers be registered. All growers must apply for a license from the Georgia Department of Agriculture. In addition, Vidalia onions can be produced only in a twenty-county area.

WRIGHTSVILLE CATFISH FESTIVAL AND TRADE SHOW • WRIGHTSVILLE

The Wrightsville Catfish Festival and Trade Show, held in April, celebrates with an arts and crafts fair, a motorcycle and antique car show, live entertainment, and, yes, they do serve catfish.

Should you like to try your hand at raising the little suckers, you can attend a seminar that will tell you everything you ever wanted to know about commercial catfish production. And then, you can browse through the trade show featuring all the equipment you'll need to start your little catfish farm.

Funny Happenings Here

The Great Locomotive Chase is one of the greatest railroad adventures of all time. James Andrews, a Union spy and contraband merchant, spent weeks gaining Confederate trust to pave the way for his plan to steal a W&ARR locomotive, destroy the track, cut telegraph lines, and burn bridges to effectively isolate Atlanta from Chattanooga.

When he and his friends boarded The General, nothing seemed amiss. But as its crew and passengers disembarked for breakfast, the band of spies struck out for Tennessee on their purloined locomotive.

Conductor William Fuller saw his train leaving, and set out to catch it, joined by his engineer and foreman. Their pursuit in a driving rain would include running on foot, pumping a hand cart, using their own abandoned switch engine, commandeering the William R. Smith, and backing all the way to Calhoun on the Texas.

At the end, Andrews ordered, "Every man for himself," and jumped train. The scoundrels were captured and tried as spies. Andrews and seven of the men were hanged and buried in unmarked graves. Eight escaped from prison, and six were paroled a year later.

But one man's scoundrel is another man's hero. In 1863, Congress awarded the Medal of Honor to Andrews' Raiders, who had been Union Soldiers. The bodies of those in unmarked graves were disinterred and buried at Chattanooga National Cemetery. Ironically, because he was a civilian, Andrews was ineligible for a medal.

Georgia Pastimes

Georgia folks have lots of ways to spend their time. Here are just a few.

THE BARE FACTS

Know the difference between naked and nekkid? According to Lewis Grizzard, naked means you ain't got no clothes on. Nekkid means you ain't got no clothes on and you're up to somethin'.

These folks are naked, and who woulda thunk it? Nudism is alive and well, right here in the middle of the Bible Belt. Georgia is home to no less than five nudist resorts, where if you're of a mind, you can romp around in the all-together. There are all sorts of resort-type activities—swimming, tennis, fishing, spas—with just that one little difference.

Check 'em out—Bare Buddics, Inc. in Lawrenceville, Bell Acre Resort in Maysville, Paradise Valley Resort in Dawsonville, Serendipity Park in Cleveland, and International Men Enjoying Nature, Inc. in Atlanta.

FOX THEATRE • ATLANTA

The Fox Theatre began life in the late 1920s as the Yaarab Temple Shrine Mosque. Serving as the headquarters for the five thousand-member Shriner's organization, it was outlandishly opulent, a grandiose monument to the excesses that marked the years before the market crash.

Its lavish exterior, complete with minarets and onion domes, was surpassed in opulence only by its interior décor. Adhering strictly to an Arabian theme, there was an indoor courtyard with a ceiling of flickering stars and drifting clouds. A striped canopy overhung the balcony, and the stage curtains, depicting mosques and Moorish rulers, glittered with hand sewn rhinestones and sequins.

The entire theatre was a masterpiece of trompe l'oiel. (We looked it up. It's a style of painting that creates an optical illusion). There were false balconies, false beams, and false tents; ornate grillwork was painted to disguise heating

The Fox Theatre offers a variety of performances, movies, and film festivals throughout the year.
Photo by Sara Foltz

ducts. Everything— –furniture, tile, men's and ladies' lounges, even the broom closets—were gilded with elaborate bronze, plaster, and painted detail.

From the beginning, the Yaarab Temple faced financial problems, which plagued it until just a few years ago. There were cost overruns (imagine that!). And then, of course, there was that pesky market crash that set off the Great Depression.

To raise additional funds, those shrewd Shriners struck a deal with movie mogul William Fox. Fox had built movie palaces in Detroit, St. Louis, and other large cities, and with a few alterations, he made the Temple into a theatre, featuring talking pictures and elaborate stage presentations.

But there was still that darn Depression. The Fox declared bankruptcy after only a few weeks. Even with a brief city ownership, it barely scraped by through the 1930s. Under new management in the 1940s, the Fox prospered, becoming one of Atlanta's finest movie houses. Occasional live entertainment by famous artists and the annual performances by the Metropolitan Opera company kept it strong through the 1960s.

The 1970s brought more hard times. Television, which kept patrons at home, and a changing movie industry that required month-long commitments on first-run films spelled trouble for the Fox. That month-long commitment was fine for the smaller theatres, which could seat only five hundred. The Fox, which sat four thousand, could complete a run in a week. It was reduced to running second-run films to a dwindling audience.

The venerable show palace was almost sold and demolished to accommodate a new Southern Bell headquarters, but Atlanta Landmarks, a non-profit organization, intervened. Through their efforts it was designated as a National Historic Landmark. It is listed on the National Register of Historic Places and is a Georgia Museum Building, the state's most prestigious ranking.

Today the Fox has been restored to its former glory and enjoys financial solvency. Movies are still shown, and there is live entertainment throughout the year. In addition, the Egyptian Ballroom and Grand Salon are rented out for a variety of events, including weddings, proms, video and film shoots, and corporate events.

Each year the Fox hosts the Summer Film Festival, which features a pre-movie sing along with Mighty Mo, the four thousand-pipe Mighty Moller theatrical organ from the theatre's early days. Patrons are assisted in the singalong by a series of slides from the 1930s that are projected onto the screen.

The prestigious theatre is located at 660 Peachtree Street, NE, in Atlanta.

TOUR DE GEORGIA

The Tour de Georgia is a 650-mile bicycle race through the rolling valleys and up the breathtaking mountains of Georgia. The event draws such international cycling champions as Italian Mario Cipolini, Germany's Jens Voight, and, yes, our own seven-time Tour de France winner Lance Armstrong. It's one of the nation's premier cycling events. Held annually the third week in April.

UNDERGROUND ATLANTA

Before Sherman made his little trek through Georgia, Atlanta already was the trade and cultural center of the South. A bustling metropolis of ten thousand, it was built along the area of the Georgia Railroad Depot, the railroad line between Atlanta and Chattanooga. Georgia had built the railroad in 1836 and placed 138 mile markers along the way. The Depot was built at the Zero Milepost, and this area—along Peachtree, Alabama, and Pryor streets—became downtown Atlanta.

After the devastation of the Civil War, Atlanta rebuilt along this same area, but by the 1920s, the burgeoning city was experiencing a severe traffic problem. To alleviate the problem, a series of concrete viaducts was built over the tracks, which elevated the street system one level. Consequently, area merchants moved their businesses to the second floor of their buildings, leaving the bottom floors for storage.

During the next forty years, Atlanta continued to spread and grow and become a hub of transportation for the nation. In 1943, a park was

Partygoers ring in a new year at Underground Atlanta's annual Peach Drop New Year's Celebration.
Courtesy of 360 Media, Inc.

built over the railroad gulch, to be replaced later by Peachtree Fountain Plaza. The area beneath the viaducts was abandoned and forgotten.

In 1968, that all changed. The area was declared an historic site, and restoration efforts began. Many of the architectural features of the storefronts, including grillwork, decorative brickwork, and carved wood posts and panels, survived and were restored to their original states. The five-block area opened in 1969. It closed in 1980, but was reopened and was once again refurbished in 1989.

Georgia Pastimes

Today, Underground Atlanta is again a thriving retail and entertainment center, chock full of family fun. You'll find retail stores and specialty and gift shops, restaurants, food vendors and cafés, and art galleries. The night life really rocks with a vast array of night clubs, and periodically, there are concerts and festivals.

If watching movies is one of your pastimes, you may have seen Georgia in the background of some of your favorites. Films shot here include *Sweet Home Alabama*, *Remember the Titans*, *Smokey and the Bandit*, *The Night the Lights Went Out in Georgia*, *My Cousin Vinny*, and *Deliverance*. Georgia's helped out on the small screen, too, with TV shows like *In the Heat of the Night* and *The Dukes of Hazzard*.

Strange But True Culture

Artists, world-class storytellers, music, and music men—it's culture with a twist in Strange But True Georgia.

Artists

Folk Artists. Self-Taught Artists. Whatever you call them, it's been said that there's just one rule in folk art: The artist must be as interesting as his art. No problem here!

HOWARD FINSTER

One man's piece of junk is another man's work of art. No one expressed this concept better than artist Howard Finster, who inscribed this quote upon one of his works:

> I took the pieces you threw away
> And put them together by night and day
> Washed by rain and dried by sun
> A million pieces all in one.

Finster, a devout Christian and Baptist minister, is known as one of the country's best folk artists. Born in 1916 in Valley Head, Alabama, he moved to Chattooga County, Georgia, in 1937, where he worked in a cotton mill in Trion. It was here that he began his creative endeavors with the construction of an outdoor museum featuring small replicas of churches and "heavenly mansions."

Finster said his work was inspired by mystical visions. In

1961, he moved to Pennville, and began construction on his "Plant Farm Museum," which involved filling in the marshy area behind his new home and constructing a natural garden. Within the garden, he placed plywood and concrete sculptures, walls, buildings, and trellises decorated with all types of manmade detritus. There were signs containing humorous, religious, and biblical texts; canals and ponds; and two metal towers constructed from bicycle and lawnmower frames.

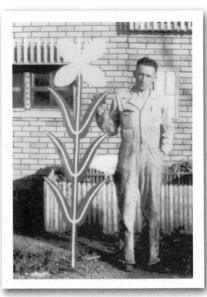

Howard Finster is known as one of the country's best folk artists.
Courtesy of Thelma Finster Bradshaw

The museum received national attention and was eventually renamed Paradise Garden. It became Finster's best known work and helped to garner numerous magazine write-ups, including one in a 1975 issue of *Esquire* and an appearance on the *The Tonight Show* in 1983.

Despite the stir his work was causing in the art world, Finster didn't quit his day job—bicycle and small-engine repair. It was while retouching the paint on a bicycle that he saw a face in a dab of paint on his finger, a sign, he said, that he was to "paint sacred art." During the late 1970s and throughout the

1980s, he produced a plethora of powerful paintings with a religious theme.

Finster's work was being displayed in prestigious art galleries, and he was often invited to lecture at universities and art schools. He even got a hand in the rock 'n' roll world by designing album covers for the Georgia rock groups Talking Heads and R.E.M.

One of the country's most prolific artists, Finster continued to produce artwork until his death at age 84 in 2001. His legacy is more than forty thousand pieces of art—paintings, sculptures, and architectural structures—that are displayed in museums and collections throughout the world. His Paradise Garden is being maintained by family and supporters and is open to the public.

BESSIE HARVEY

As a folk artist, Bessie Harvey got to the root of the matter. Harvey, who died in 1994, created dolls using tree roots and branches, to which she often added glitter, beads, and strands of her own hair.

Harvey began making her dolls as a relief from the strife of being the wife of an abusive alcoholic man. She said she often meditated while creating and made a communion with God through her artwork.

LANIER MEADERS

Lanier Meaders, grandson of Meaders Pottery founder John Milton Meaders, is considered one of the country's most gifted Southern potters. His distinctive style is often credited with single-handedly rescuing the art of Southern folk pottery.

Lanier was partial to the old forms of pots, jars, and churns used in everyday life. He was especially fond of the jugs used to hold moonshine. During Prohibition, the creation of these jugs kept many potters in business.

Although he loved making these practical wares, Lanier knew the survival of his craft depended upon the creation of pottery for a broader audience. He began producing the popular face jug—a jug shaped as a face or head with eyes, nose, and teeth. The pieces could be either humorous or foreboding, and Lanier became the foremost producer of this art form.

Lanier's face jugs and other artwork are sought by collectors throughout the country and are featured in the Smithsonian Institute and other museums. He was awarded the National Heritage Fellowship by the National Endowment for the Arts and received the Governor's Award for the Arts in Georgia in 1987. He died in 1998.

R.A. MILLER

Like many folk artists, Ruben A. Miller didn't discover his talent until the later years of his life. Born in 1912 in the house where he lives today, he worked in cotton mills, farmed, and preached at the Free Will Baptist Church.

When glaucoma stole most of his eyesight by age sixty-five, Miller retired from preaching and began creating. He covered the hill near his home with hundreds of windmills—whirligigs, he called them—festooned with animal or human shapes snipped from tin.

The hill of whirligigs attracted local attention, and in 1984, the Georgia rock group R.E.M filmed a video there. After that, folk artists from far and wide streamed into Rabbittown,

R.A. Miller first displayed his whirligigs on a hill near his home.
Photo by Randy Franklin

prompting Miller to experiment further. He began producing a variety of crude wooden and tin animal and human shapes, which he posted around his yard. His favorite animal images include birds, dogs, pigs, and snakes. The human images include icons, such as Elvis and Uncle Sam, devils, and angels. One abiding figure is the "Blow Oskar," inspired by his cousin Oskar, who blew his horn every time he passed Miller's home. In addition to the windmills and cutouts, Miller produces paintings and drawings with the same themes.

For more than twenty years, folk art collectors have flocked to tiny Rabbittown to buy Miller's work, and art critics throughout the country have raved about the complexity beneath his deceptively simple art. Despite the attention, Miller remains pragmatic, remarking that "they don't know it ain't nothing but junk."

Strange But True Culture

NELLIE MAE ROWE

After a lifetime as a farmhand and domestic worker, Nellie Mae Rowe began a new life as a folk artist. She decorated her home—not far from the governor's mansion—with a display of bright drawings, stuffed dolls wearing wigs and glasses, plastic flowers, sculptures made of hardened chewing gum, and Christmas ornaments.

Many of her neighbors didn't appreciate Rowe's decorating style, but folk art collectors soon began flocking in for a visit. Rowe was always happy to give a tour of her home and treat her visitors to a round of gospel singing, accompanying herself on an electric organ.

Like most folk artists, Rowe used simple materials, such as crayons, markers, paper, cardboard, and egg cartons. She also created figures and dolls from recycled items (really recycled!), such as ABC gum (Already Been Chewed!) and fabric scraps. She embellished her work with trinkets, marbles, and plastic toys.

Rowe died in 1982, but her work is exhibited in many museums, including the Smithsonian American Art Museum, The Library of Congress American Folklife Center, and the American Folk Art Museum in New York.

HARRY TEAGUE

Hard times affect people differently. For some the hard times become a hammer that beats them down. Others take that hammer and beat the hard times into art that touches the world.

Harry Teague is one that didn't let the hard times beat him

down. When at age forty-six a stroke paralyzed his right side and took away his ability to read and speak, Teague simply picked up a paint brush and began talking through art. Despite the adversity he

Harry Teague speaks to the world through his art.
Courtesy of Harry and Diannia Teague

faces, Teague's bright, colorful paintings are filled with wit, humor, and irony, and though his voice is silenced, he often uses his art to make strong social statements.

Inventors

Georgia is full of innovative people. Here's just a sample of them and their inventions.

Charles W. Buggs

Maybe it was his name that gave Charles Buggs his interest in germs. Buggs, a scientist from Brunswick, conducted important research on why some bacteria do not react to certain medications. In 1944, he wrote several articles outlining his ideas on penicillin and skin grafting, and the value of chemicals in treating bone fractures. His research on how to use antibiotics to prevent and cure disease helped give the world a better understanding of how medicines can heal.

CLARENCE W. ELDER

Born in Georgia in 1935, Clarence Elder moved to Baltimore, Maryland, and opened Elder Systems Incorporated, a research and development company. In 1976, he invented Occustat, a monitoring and energy conservation control system. The system is designed to reduce energy use in temporarily vacant buildings, such as schools and hotels.

Consisting of energy units connected by an electronic beam aimed at the building's entrance, Occustat monitors incoming and outgoing traffic. Once the building is empty, the beam activates the system, which then reduces heat and light demand. The system has been shown to boost energy savings by 30 percent.

DR. CRAWFORD W. LONG

Folks in the mid-1800s must've really been bored. Back then, one of the biggest fads was "ether parties," where partygoers sniffed the anesthetic in an effort to get high. OK, so maybe they weren't any more bored than partygoers today. Anyway, sometimes they'd sniff a bit too much and would pass out.

Jefferson physician Crawford Long noticed that when the partiers passed out and fell, they often experienced cuts or bruises, but felt no pain and had no memory of receiving them. A compassionate country doctor who hated causing his patients pain, Crawford thought, Hmmm…what if…?

On March 30, 1842, he placed an ether-soaked handkerchief

over the face of James Venable, a Jefferson citizen who had several tumors on his neck that needed to be removed. Before he could count to ten, Venable was sound asleep, and Long removed the tumors. When Venable awoke, he had no memory of the surgery. Thus went the first ever surgery using anesthesia—for which Long charged the exorbitant sum of $2.00.

Although the surgery was witnessed by several medical students, Long unfortunately wasn't much for writing, and so neglected to publish his accomplishment. Some Boston physicians eventually hit upon the advantages of ether, and, no slouches in the publicity department, they published the account of their surgery in October 1846. By that time, Long had performed several more ether-assisted operations.

Interested in knowing more? Then visit the Crawford W. Long Museum, which contains a diorama of Venable's historic surgery. The museum is located at 28 College Street in Jefferson.

DR. JOHN S. PEMBERTON

When you are enjoying a cold Coca-Cola at your favorite ballpark, thank John Pemberton for inventing what has become the world's best-selling soft drink. But though it was his most famous—and profitable—concoction, he had a hand in other innovations as well.

Before Coca-Cola, Pemberton concocted a drink called French Wine Coca, which contained wine, caffeine, and an extract of cocaine. It was when Prohibition nixed the wine ingredient that Pemberton came up with the formula for Coca-Cola, which still contained cocaine and caffeine.

Though at that time, most people were unaware of cocaine's addicting properties, Pemberton, a physician, chemist, and pharmacist, was personally familiar with them. A lieutenant colonel who served with distinction in the Confederate Army, Pemberton was wounded in the fighting at Columbus in April 1865.

Strange But True: The Coca-Cola Company would not grant permission for the inclusion of the image of Dr. John Pemberton that appears on the Coca-Cola Heritage Home Page.

To alleviate the pain, he prescribed himself morphine and cocaine and became addicted to both. It's believed by some that he purposely included cocaine in his drinks to addict his customers and thereby boost sales.

Despite his weaknesses, Pemberton was well-respected as a physician and a chemist. In addition to concocting drinks, he established J.S. Pemberton and Company of Columbus, a series of analytical and manufacturing laboratories. The company manufactured pharmaceutical and chemical preparations used in all types of applications.

Converted into the state's first testing labs and staffed by Pemberton's best scientists, these labs played a major role in eliminating the sale of fraudulent agricultural chemicals and helped to ensure prosecution of the sellers. Pemberton's labs are still in operation as part of the Georgia Department of Agriculture.

XAVIER ROBERTS

Remember we told you abut Babyland, the hospital for Cabbage Patch Kids? Well, now we're going to tell you who to thank for the birth of those ugly little dolls. It all began in 1976, when Xavier Roberts, a 21-year-old art student "rediscovered" needle molding, an early 1800s German technique of fabric sculpting.

Roberts, who was working his way through school managing the Unicoi Craft Shop in Helen, combined his interest in sculpture with the quilting skills passed down from his mother. He sewed up a group of dolls he called Little People and came up with the marketing concept to require "adoption" of the dolls and inclusion of a birth certificate with each doll. His doll "Dexter" won first place for sculpture in the 1978 Osceola Art Show in Kissimmee, Florida.

Traveling the Southeast, Roberts exhibited his handmade originals at arts and crafts shows, and found that people were willing, even eager, to pay the $30 to $40 "adoption fee" for the dolls. When he returned to Georgia, he recruited five school buddies and began the Original Appalachian Artworks, Inc. Renovating a former medical facility in Cleveland, they opened the Babyland General Hospital, where the public could witness the "birth" of their dolls.

After signing an agreement with a toy manufacturer to produce replicas of the dolls, Roberts changed the name of the Little People dolls. As a child, his parents had told him that he was found in a cabbage patch to avoid questions about the birds and bees, and so, he named his dolls the Cabbage Patch Kids.

The dolls share one of the most successful stories in the history of toy manufacturing. In reaction to the "adoption" frenzy of the 1980s, the dolls were named the official mascot for the 1992 and 1996 U.S. Olympic Teams and were selected by a nationwide vote as one of fifteen icons to be placed on a U.S. postage stamp commemorating the 1980s in the USPS's Celebrate the Century stamp program.

ELI WHITNEY

Eli Whitney left New England for the Deep South in 1792. A recent graduate of Yale, he had wanted to study law, but found he must first pay off some debts. The most lucrative job he could find was that of a private tutor on the plantation of Nathaniel Greene.

While there, Whitney noted that plantation owners were struggling to make a profit from their cotton crops. The problem, it seemed, was the fact that cotton seeds were sticky and hard to remove, which inhibited the commercial production of cotton.

With the encouragement and financial support of Nathaniel's wife, Catherine, Whitney set about inventing a machine that could quickly remove the seeds. He believed that if he could invent a machine that he could patent, he could become a wealthy man.

He did invent the cotton gin and obtain a fourteen-year patent on the machine. But instead of building the machines and selling them to the farmers, Whitney and his business partner, Phineas Miller, opted to place as many gins as possible throughout the South and charge farmers a fee of two-fifths the profit for doing the ginning for them.

Angered at what they considered too high a fee, the farmers

began making their own versions of the gin, claiming them as new inventions. Although they brought suit against the farmers, because of a loophole in the patent law, Whitney and Miller were unable to win any suits. The two never made any big profits from the cotton gin.

The South, however, profited immensely from Whitney's invention. The yield of raw cotton doubled each decade after 1800. Other inventions, such as machines to spin and weave the cotton and steamboats to transport it, fueled demand. By mid-century, America was supplying three-quarters of the world's cotton.

Despite the cotton gin fiasco, Whitney eventually did become a wealthy man from his ingenuity. In 1798, he came up with a way to manufacture muskets by machine so that the parts were interchangeable, making him the father of the mass production method.

Eli Whitney is credited with inventing the cotton gin, but many believe that the ideas behind his machine came from his employer and benefactor Catherine Greene.

Music From The Heart

Ray Charles. Lena Horne. Brenda Lee. Little Richard. Chet Atkins. Otis Redding. Gladys Knight and the Pips. The Tams. The B-52's. Usher. Georgia has been rocking the world for decades. But these folks and their music are well-known and nowhere near as interesting as our Strange But True Georgia music and the people who make it.

Strange But True Culture

FIDDLIN' JOHN CARSON

A native of Fannin County, Fiddlin' John Carson is credited with launching the country music recording industry. Carson was born in Blue Ridge in 1868. In his early years, he made a living variously as a farmer, a jockey, a railroad worker, and a moonshiner, playing his fiddle and singing on the side.

By 1913, he had become a favorite at fiddling contests, where he played and sang songs that appealed to the mostly rural audience—songs about hard times, moonshining, and spending time in jail.

Carson was a 54-year-old housepainter when he walked into the Atlanta's WSB, the South's first radio station, and requested air time. He stepped up to the microphone and began playing his mountain music, fiddling and singing until exhaustion set in. Listener reaction was overwhelmingly positive, and Carson became a regular performer on WSB throughout the 1930s and 1940s.

In 1923, an official with a New York recording company was visiting Atlanta. No fan of Carson's music, he nevertheless

Fiddlin' John Carson is credited with launching country music's recording industry.
Courtesy of the Georgia Music Hall of Fame and Museum

allowed Carson to record two songs, "The Little Old Log Cabin in the Lane" and "The Old Hen Cackled and the Rooster's Going to Crow."

The initial supply of five hundred records sold out quickly, and when sales reached five hundred thousand, the New York record executives decided this country music thing sounded pretty good after all. They called Carson to New York to make more records of his old-time ballads and fiddlin' tunes, thereby launching the country music recording industry.

Carson recorded 165 songs in all, often accompanied by his daughter, Rosa Lee, who became a performer in her own right. Carson spent his last years as an elevator operator in the Georgia state capitol. He was inducted into the Georgia Music Hall of Fame in 1984.

PEG LEG HOWELL

Joshua Barnes Howell was born in Eatonton in 1888. The child of farmers, Howell was around music all his life, but showed no interest until age twenty-one, when he picked up the guitar one night and "stayed up until he learned it."

He worked the family farm alongside his father and played guitar on the side until a life-changing event occurred. During an altercation with his brother-in-law, Howell was shot in the right leg. As a result, he lost his leg and gained a nickname.

No longer able to work the farm, he worked various jobs, but nothing regularly. In 1923, he moved to Atlanta, where he formed the blues group Peg Leg Howell and His Gang. To help with expenses, Howell began selling bootleg whiskey, and in

1925, the revenuers caught up with him. He spent a few months in prison, but by November 1926, he was out, playing his music on the streets of Atlanta. At this time, Columbia Records was sending representatives to the South twice a year to record blues artists. They recorded Howell singing "New Prison Blues," a song he'd learned during his unfortunate incarceration.

Columbia Records recorded Howell—along with his gang—for the next two years. The April 1929 session was Howell's last. Through the next years, he took on various jobs and continued to play the streets of Atlanta whenever he needed money.

In 1952, Howell lost his left leg to diabetes, and, confined to a wheelchair, he lived on welfare. In 1963, he enjoyed a short-lived revival, when Testament Records recorded him one last time. Howell died in 1966. His musical legacy was building a bridge between plantation work songs and traditional blues music.

BLIND WILLIE MCTELL

Born in Thomson in 1901, William Samuel McTell, best known as Blind Willie McTell, was considered one of the best guitarists and storytellers in blues history. He was one of the great blues musicians of the 1920s and 1930s.

McTell lost his sight in late childhood and attended schools for the blind in Georgia, New York, and Michigan. He learned to play the guitar from his mother in his early teens, and after her death, he left home to tour in carnivals and medicine shows. In the 1920s and 1930s, he traveled between

Atlanta, Augusta, Savannah, and Macon, a region that encompassed the lighter rhythms and ragtime influence of the Eastern Seaboard/ Piedmont style, and the Deep South style, with its intense rhythms.

McTell's recording career began in 1927, when he began recording for Victor Records and continued in 1928 for Columbia Records. These recording sessions produced the blues classics "Statesboro Blues," "Mama 'Tain't Long for Day," and "Georgia Rag."

Throughout his recording career, McTell recorded for numerous labels, and under various names. For Okeh Records, he was Georgia Bill. He was Blind Willie for Vocalion, and Red Hot Willie Glaze for Bluebird, just to name a few.

In 1983, Bob Dylan honored McTell with his "Blind Willie McTell," in which he said no one could play the blues like

After losing his eyesight in late childhood, Blind Willie learned to play the guitar as a teenager.
Courtesy of the Georgia Music Hall of Fame and Museum

Blind Willie McTell. McTell was inducted into the Blue Foundation's Blues Hall of Fame in 1981 and into the Georgia

Music Hall of Fame in 1990. Every year, his hometown of Thomson hosts a Blind Willie McTell Festival in his honor.

SACRED HARP MUSIC

Although Sacred Harp music's origins in the U.S. lie in colonial New England, Georgia and Alabama are now the acknowledged cultural centers for this centuries-old musical form. Every year enthusiasts from all over the world travel to Carrollton to attend the Chattahoochee Musical Convention, which was begun in 1852 and is the country's oldest functioning convention.

If you've never heard of Sacred Harp music, the first thing you should know is: There's no harp. In fact, the only instruments used in Sacred Harp music are the singers' voices, and they are LOUD, so loud that the music is sometimes called Loud Hymns. It's also called fasola music for the notes sung, and shaped-note music because of the unique shape of the printed notes.

The Sacred Harp tradition began in Georgia with Benjamin Franklin White and Elisha J. King. White and King, Hamilton County singing teachers, together compiled, transcribed, and composed a book of 250 Sacred Harp tunes. Their book, *The Sacred Harp*, was published in 1844.

The publication of this book sparked an interest in Sacred Harp music, and White was instrumental in guiding the growth of that interest. (King had died shortly after publication.) He organized singing schools and taught shaped-note singing, using *The Sacred Harp* as the official songbook.

To help ensure the future of Sacred Harp music, White organized the first ever permanent singing convention at Huntersville. The Southern Musical Convention was established in 1845 and was held annually for the next twenty years in nine different Georgia counties. Its success sparked the formation of the Chattahoochee Musical Convention.

Scholars have written extensively about *The Sacred Harp* and its influence on the spread of Sacred Harp music throughout the country. White's third revision of the songbook, which contains 573 songs, is considered the bible of Sacred Harp music and is still used today.

GID TANNER AND HIS SKILLET LICKERS

John Gideon Tanner, a redheaded chicken farmer from Thomas Bridge, learned to play the fiddle as a teenager. He was quite good at it, too, becoming a regular participant in the Georgia Old-Time Fiddlers' Conventions, held annually in Atlanta between 1913 and 1935.

Tanner was an audience favorite, entertaining the crowds with his skillful fiddling, his legendary voice range, and his comedic talents. He reportedly knew the words and music to two thousand songs, many of them comic. His performance of comedic songs, such as "I'm Satisfied," always brought down the house, and spread his fame as far as New York.

In 1924, just months after fellow Georgian Fiddlin' John Carson made his first recordings for the Okeh label, Columbia came callin'. They wanted Tanner to come to New York and record some of his fiddlin' songs. Tanner brought along friend and contest partner, the blind guitarist Riley Puckett, who was also a talented singer. Together, they recorded some of the first southern fiddle and guitar songs.

Two years later, Columbia executive Frank Walker came to Atlanta to record Southern performers. With the advent of the new electrical recording process, Walker was searching for a

Gid Tanner and His Skillet Lickers bridged the gap between traditional folk music and modern pop.
Courtesy of the Georgia Music Hall of Fame and Museum

fuller sound than past recordings. He asked Tanner and Puckett to join forces with fiddler Clayton McMichen and Fate Norris on the mandolin and harmonica.

Under the name Gid Tanner and His Skillet Lickers, the new group produced the whopper hits "Bully of the Town" and "Pass Around the Bottle and We'll All Take A Drink." The next year, they came up with a new innovation—recordings of comedy skits, which combined music with dialogue. The skits usually portrayed band members as moonshiners who were always "making a little brew and drinking a little brew." The skit records outsold the group's straight records.

There was dissension among the band members almost from the start, and during the eight years the group recorded, some members left and new ones were added. Despite that, the group remained popular. Their last recording, "Down Yonder," recorded in 1934, was the group's biggest seller.

Gid Tanner and His Skillet Lickers are credited with bridging the gap between traditional folk music and modern pop. Tanner himself left a living legacy. Both his grandson, Phil, and his great-grandson, Russell, are fiddlers performing in an old-time fiddling band called the Skillet Lickers. Tanner was inducted into the Georgia Music Hall of Fame in 1988.

Writers

No doubt about it, Georgia is a hotbed of literary talent. Nationally known sons and daughters include Flannery O'Conner, James Dickey, Margaret Mitchell, and Pat Conroy. Here are just a few more who require a mention on our Strange But True Georgia tour.

ELIAS BOUDINOT

Galagina "Buck" Watie was born in 1804 to a changing world for the Cherokee Nation. His father, Oo-watie, a Cherokee leader, had begun to follow the U.S. Indian policy that encouraged Native Americans to become "culturally white" by farming, learning to read and write, and converting to Christianity.

Galagina was sent to a Christian school, where he so excelled that he was invited to attend the Foreign Mission School in Cornwall, Connecticut. While traveling there, he stopped to visit Elias Boudinot, who had served in the Continental Congress. He was so impressed with Boudinot, that to honor him, he decided to take his name.

Boudinot (Watie) excelled at Cornwall as well, and the faculty arranged for him to enter Andover Theological Seminary. Bad health, unfortunately, made that impossible, and Boudinot returned to Georgia, much encouraged by his experience in the white man's world.

That encouragement was diminished, however, by the outcry that ensued Boudinot's marriage to the daughter of a Cornwall physician. Agents of the Foreign Mission School called the marriage criminal and closed the school.

Despite his doubts that Native Americans would ever be accepted as equals, Boudinot became a proponent of the government's "civilization" program. As a clerk of the Cherokee Council, he helped to write a republican constitution patterned after that of the U.S. and participated in Bible and temperance societies.

As founding editor of *The Cherokee Phoenix*, the first Native American newspaper, Boudinot became one of the most ardent and eloquent defenders of Cherokee rights. Addressing his readers in both English and the language of the Cherokee, he denounced Georgia's "Indian Laws," which refused to acknowledge the sovereignty of the Cherokee nation, thereby allowing their lands to be claimed by white settlers and requiring any white men living in the Cherokee Nation to declare an oath of allegiance to Georgia. Boudinot also addressed the Indian Removal Act, passed by Congress in 1830, which advocated moving the Cherokee Nation to Indian Territory—now the state of Oklahoma.

In 1832, the Supreme Court ruled in favor of the Cherokee Nation, recognizing its sovereignty and declaring the Removal Laws invalid. The Cherokee would have to agree to removal, and the treaty would have to be ratified by the Senate.

When the state of Georgia refused to repeal their laws, and the federal government refused to make the state comply, Boudinot became discouraged. He came to believe that to emigrate as a nation to the Indian Territory was better than the extinction the Cherokee Nation faced if they stayed, a stance that put him at odds with the *Phoenix*'s publishers.

Elias Boudinot was the founding editor of the first Native American newspaper, *The Cherokee Phoenix.*
Courtesy of Paul Ridenour

He resigned his editorship, and with a few like-minded Cherokee formed a Treaty Party. In 1835, despite the fact that they had no authority to do so, the members of the party signed a treaty with the government. The treaty, known as the

1835 Treaty of New Echota, was pushed through the Senate, and in 1838, the Cherokee made their long, agonizing trek along the Trail of Tears to their new home in the West.

Boudinot and his fellow signers were sentenced to death as traitors by the Cherokee. In 1839, as he stepped from his new home in Oklahoma, a group of men attacked and killed him. His uncle and cousin, who also signed the treaty, were killed the same day.

ERSKINE CALDWELL

That Erskine Caldwell. He sure was a bad boy. All them things he wrote in his books. Why, Edna Mae, it just weren't fittin'!

Those words, more or less, echoed around the country when White Oak native Erskine Caldwell hit the literary scene. His works were banned from libraries, and he fought the court—and won—on obscenity charges against his second novel, *God's Little Acre*. He, more than any other author of his time, fought censorship of his work.

Much of the hew and cry came from Southerners who saw betrayal in Caldwell's frank depictions of the South. Well, you know what they say: You gotta write about what you know. That's just what Caldwell did. Sometimes called the "master of ribaldry," he wrote graphic novels and short stories about the family relations of Georgia's poor.

As the son of a Presbyterian minister who moved from church to church, Caldwell saw much of the South during his formative years. The family rarely lived in one place more than six months, and it was during this time that Caldwell came to know the life of the Southern sharecropper, a subject he dissected in his first novel, *Tobacco Road*.

These first two novels are by far the most well-known. Both were made into movies and adapted into Broadway plays, with *Tobacco Road* having the distinction of becoming one of the longest running plays in history. This novel was included in The Modern Library's list of the one hundred most influential novels since 1900. More than fourteen million copies of *God's Little Acre* have been sold. In all, Caldwell published twenty-six novels, sixteen collections of stories, fifteen non-fiction books, two children's books, and a collection of poetry.

Although many Southerners decried Caldwell's depiction of sharecroppers, he worked tirelessly to change the tenant system. His attacks on this system in the *New York Post* and a collaborative work with his wife, photographer Margaret Bourke White, titled *You Have Seen Their Faces*, helped lead to New Deal-era reforms.

Despite the controversy over his work, literary critics considered Caldwell a literary realist and sociologist, ranking him alongside such literary greats as F. Scott Fitzgerald, Thomas Wolfe, John Steinbeck, and William Faulkner. The controversy never hurt sales. By the late 1940s, he had sold more books than any writer in national history. In 1984, he was nominated to the American Academy of Arts and Letters, three years before his death in 1987.

HARRY CREWS

Like those of other Georgia writers, many of Harry Crews's works are set in the rural South. The difference lies in Crews's personal fascination with physical freaks and an equal obsession with physical perfection and the beauty of athletic prowess.

These themes often come together, as in *The Gypsy's Curse*, his novel about a musclebound midget, and in *The Body* about professional bodybuilders. In other works portraying football players, dog fighters, snake hunters, and weight lifters, the beauty of athleticism is taken to freakish levels.

These recurring themes in Crews's writing stem, no doubt, from his childhood. He was born in 1935 in Bacon County to indigent farmers, working to dig a living out of dirt-poor Georgia.

When he was five, Crews contracted polio, a disease that caused the muscles in his legs to contract, drawing his heels up to the back of his legs and rendering him unable to walk for six weeks. When the cramps subsided, he conditioned himself to walk again by pulling himself along a fence line, which strengthened his atrophied muscles.

Not long after, Crews was playing outside on a day when his mother was preparing pigs that had been slaughtered. Somehow, Crews fell into a pot of boiling water used to remove hair from the pigs. He was pulled from the pot and set next to it. The incident was described in his autobiography *A Childhood: The Biography of a Place*: "I reached over and touched my right hand with my left, and the whole thing came off like a wet glove. I mean the skin on the top of the wrist and the back of my hand, along with the fingernails, all just turned loose and slid down to the ground. I could see my fingernails lying in the little puddle my flesh made on the ground in front of me."

As an adult, Crews became obsessed with learning to

write, an obsession, he says, that cost him his family. It seems he learned. *The Gospel Singer*, Crews's first novel, was published in 1968, and he published a book a year for the next seven years. His work has been compared to that of William Faulkner and Flannery O'Conner in that they are written in the Southern Gothic tradition. He was given an NEA grant, won an award from the American Academy of Arts and Letters, and in 1977 won an award from the Coordinating Council of Literary Magazines for the best non-fiction piece published in a literary magazine.

JOEL CHANDLER HARRIS

Joel Chandler Harris, author of *Tales of Uncle Remus* and many other books and stories, was born in Eatonton in 1845 and grew up there. As a teen, he began work as a printing compositor for Joseph Turner, a local plantation owner and publisher of *The Countryman*, the country's only plantation newspaper. Harris's job here profoundly enriched his future and America's literature. With full access to the plantation's slave quarters, he spent hours listening to the animal stories told by Uncle George Terrell, Old Harbert, and Aunt Crissy, who became models for his later stories. It was here that he developed an uncanny knack for writing in dialect.

Harris's stories of Uncle Remus and the gang were wildly popular when first published in 1880, making him second only in fame to Mark Twain. The stories—and Harris—fell out of favor later, and were often banned as racist by people who took exception to the obvious portrayal of blacks as animals and the black rural dialect. These folks completely missed Harris's allegorical intent to show the powerless, enslaved by law but freed by an agile mind, outsmarting the powerful.

Perhaps more enlightened times have finally prevailed, however. Harris and his wily characters have recently regained some of the respect they deserve as literary figures. Though some animosity toward the stories remains—as evidenced by fellow

Joel Chandler Harris, author of *Tales of Uncle Remus*, was born in Eatonton.
Courtesy of Hargrett Rare Book & Manuscript Library/University of Georgia Libraries

Eatontonian Alice Walker's comment that they stole part of her childhood by making her feel ashamed—the books have been restored to the shelves, and Eatonton proudly honors Harris as a favored son with the Uncle Remus Museum and the restoration of his family home.

ALICE WALKER

Alice Walker was born in Eatonton in 1944, the daughter of a sharecropper and a part-time seamstress. By all accounts, Walker was a precocious child in her early years. She began school at age four. She had an adventurous soul and an outgoing personality. That changed when, at the age of eight, she was blinded in one eye by her brother, who accidentally shot her with a BB gun.

The eye developed a large white cataract, a scar for which Walker was mercilessly teased. Embarrassed, she became shy and withdrawn, afraid to look others in the eye for fear of being ridiculed. During these young years, she spent much time reading, and she began to write poetry as a way of dealing with her difficulties. Although later surgery removed the hated scar and helped to restore her former equanimity, she credits this time as an outcast with enabling her to see past the physical and see people and situations as they really are.

Alice Walker helped Eatonton become known as the Literary Capital of the South.
Courtesy of University of North Carolina at Chapel Hill

Walker published her first work, a short story entitled "To Hell with Dying," in 1967. Her first book, *The Third Life of Grange Copeland*, received criticism because of her unflattering portrait of the African-American male, which many thought exaggerated. Walker denied the claim, saying she'd witnessed this behavior first-hand, and would continue to portray it as she had lived it.

Walker is recognized as a leading voice in literature. Her works frankly address racism and sexism, twin afflictions that continue to impact African-Americans, and seek to preserve the black culture. Her women characters are strong and resourceful in overcoming the oppression they face from society and their own culture.

The Color Purple, Walker's third book, carried these themes throughout. Made into an Oscar award-winning movie, it garnered Walker international fame and brought insight into black culture.

Historical Events Around Georgia

From the Revolutionary War to Pioneer days to the Civil War, Georgians love to take a step back in time and re-live the old days.

Civil War Reenactments

Georgia has more Civil War reenactments than Carter's got liver pills. Could it be we think if we keep redoing it, one day we'll chase those damn Yankees back over the Mason-Dixon Line? Nah. It's just a good excuse to dress up in old clothes and play soldier. Here's just a mere sample of the state's yearly reenactments.

BATTLE FOR ATLANTA • CONYERS
Every year in November, the town of Conyers takes a step back in time and relives the days of the Civil War. In a three-day celebration, Civil War reenactors from around the country gather for the event, which features Confederate and Union troops in authentic Civil War Uniforms. Every day, the reenactors stage key battles of the Atlanta campaign, complete with mounted cavalry charges and marching troops. They have a dress parade, drill competitions, and a tea for the ladies.

The event is held at the Georgia International Horse Park.

BATTLE OF CHICKAMAUGA • FORT OGLETHORPE
Victory for the Rebs in the Battle of Chickamauga, fought on

Historical Events Around Georgia

September 19 and 20, 1863, marked the end of the Union's Chickamauga campaign. It was the most significant defeat for the Union's offensive in south-central Tennessee and northwestern Georgia.

Chickamauga, which is Native American for River of Death, lived up to its name that bloody September. The two-day battle took the lives of 16,170 Union soldiers and 18,454 Confederates.

A national park has been established at the Chickamauga Battlefield, which also commemorates the Battle of Chattanooga. The first of its kind in the nation, the park celebrated its one hundreth birthday in 1990. A seven-mile tour of the park takes visitors through key points in the battlefield. A reenactment is held in September each year.

BATTLE OF JONESBOROUGH • JONESBORO
Fought on August 31 and September 1, 1864, the Battle of Jonesborough was one of General Hood's ill-advised attacks in the Atlanta Campaign and was the final battle that caused Atlanta to fall to the Union.

Artillery reenactment unit in midst of the Battle of Jonesborough.
Photo by Judi H. Peterson/Historical Jonesboro

A reenactment of the Battle of Jonesborough is held annually at the Stately Oaks Plantation in Jonesboro. In addition to battle reenactments, events include a living history demonstration, authentic soldier competitions, shooting contests, fiddle and string band competitions, and food vendors.

BATTLE OF KENNESAW MOUNTAIN • KENNESAW

The Battle of Kennesaw Mountain was fought on June 27, 1864. All through spring and early summer, Sherman had been pursuing Confederate General Joseph Johnston, trying to draw him out in the open for a fight.

Despite fierce fighting on this day, the Union troops were unable to dislodge the Rebels from their mountain haven, and Johnston handed Sherman one of the few Union defeats in the Atlanta Campaign.

A park has been established on the Kennesaw battlefield. A reenactment is held annually and other Civil War events are held throughout the year.

BATTLE OF RESACA • RESACA

The Battle of Resaca, fought May 14 and 15, 1864, was the first major battle of the Atlanta Campaign. It is reenacted every year by the volunteers of the Georgia Division Reenactors Association, one of the nation's oldest Civil War reenactment groups. Other activities include camping, attending a social, and dancing to music provided by the 52nd Tennessee Regimental String band. A Memorial Service is conducted at the Resaca Confederate Cemetery, where 450 soldiers were laid to rest.

Historical Events Around Georgia

Battle of Tunnel Hill • Tunnel Hill

The tunnel of Tunnel Hill was a vital passage on the Western and Atlantic Railroad's line from Atlanta to Chattanooga. The engineering marvel of its time, the tunnel was built by two separate companies that started on either side of Georgia's Chetoogetta Mountain and met in the middle. The tunnel is 1,477 feet long and was the first tunnel built south of the Mason-Dixon line.

Construction began in 1848, and immediately, a town sprang up to service the needs of train passengers and the construction crews. Incorporated as Tunnelsville in 1848, the town was later renamed Tunnel Hill.

Tunnel Hill was a beehive of activity during the Civil War. Goods and supplies for the Confederacy had to pass through the tunnel, making it a vital entity to both sides. Control of the tunnel was contested several times in 1864.

During the battle of Chickamauga, Tunnel Hill's Clisby-Austin House served as a Confederate hospital. When General John Hood's leg was amputated during battle, both he and his leg were sent here, with the idea that, should he die, his leg could be buried with him. The leg, it seems, is buried in the family cemetery near the house.

General Sherman began his Atlanta Campaign here by routing the Confederates who had camped here after the battles around Chattanooga. On May 7, 1864, he seized the tunnel and established his headquarters in the Clisby-Austin House.

A bigger and more modern tunnel was built in the late 1920s, and for many years the original tunnel sat dormant, covered in kudzu. A recent effort by Tunnel Hill citizens helped to restore the tunnel and established a museum nearby. Both are now open for tours during reenactments.

The yearly events, held the first weekend after Labor Day, feature battle reenactments and camping on the original battle sites, including the Clisby-Austin plantation, which still stands. With more than fifteen hundred participants, the battles are fought by soldiers in Civil War uniforms using authentic artillery. There is a ball where guests get the opportunity to dress up like Scarlett and Rhett, and museum and tunnel tours. Living history demonstrations are held for area school children on Fridays.

Georgia joined the Confederacy on January 19, 1861.

BATTLE OF WAYNESBOROUGH • WAYNESBORO

The Battle of Waynesborough was actually a series of running cavalry battles between Union General Judson Kilpatrick and the Reb's Fighting Joe Wheeler in late November and early December 1864. Atlanta had fallen in September, and Sherman had his sights set on Savannah—the last stop on his March to the Sea.

The wily Sherman conceived a plan to pretend Macon was the next target of his left wing and Augusta the target of his right wing, causing the Confederates to amass their diminished forces to defend those cities.

Historical Events Around Georgia

Sherman's ruse worked handily. With a contingent of ten thousand, General Braxton Bragg waited for the Union arrival in Augusta just twenty-five miles north of Waynesborough. But, of course, that arrival never came. Kilpatrick and his left wing brigades quietly took Savannah on December 22, 1864. A telegraph from Sherman to President Lincoln presented "as a Christmas gift, the City of Savannah...."

Reenactments of the Battle of Waynesborough are held annually in December, where there's fightin' and dancin' and paradin'.

Living History

If the Civil War isn't far enough back in time for you, don't despair! There's plenty more Georgia history to relive.

BATTLES OF BLOODY MARSH AND GULLY HOLE CREEK • ST. SIMON'S ISLAND

The British colony of Georgia was founded in 1733 by General James Oglethorpe. Aware that the Spanish considered the area part of their territory, he built two forts on St. Simon's Island. Fort St. Simon's was built at the mouth of the Frederica River, where invading forces would have to pass before reaching the inland Fort Frederica. Turns out this was an astute decision.

In 1740, Oglethorpe launched an attempt to wrest St. Augustine, Florida, from the Spanish. When the land grab failed, he returned to Frederica to bolster his defenses for an anticipated counterattack.

The attack came two years later when Spanish forces landed on the coast of St. Simon's Island and advanced on Fort St. Simon's, which they captured and used as their base of operations. On July 7, 1742, Don Manuel de Montiano, Governor of Florida and leader of the invasion, sent out a scouting party. As the party approached Fort Frederica, Oglethorpe, a ragtag band of British Rangers, allied Yamacraw Indians, and Scottish Highlanders engaged them in a skirmish, later named the Battle of Gully Hole Creek. During the hand-to-hand combat, many of the Spanish forces broke and ran back to Fort St. Simon's.

The Spanish fled south, with Oglethorpe in hot pursuit. He halted the chase at an advantageous piece of ground, where he was joined by a regiment of British Regulars. Posting the regiment and the Highlanders along the edge of a marshy area, which the Spanish would have to pass to reach Frederica, he returned to Fort Frederica to gather more forces.

Meanwhile, Montiano sent out a force to rescue battle survivors. The troops were ambushed by the British, and the two battled across the marsh. Many British soldiers turned tail and ran, only to be caught by Oglethorpe on his way back. He ordered the men to return, but by the time he and the deserters got back, the not-so-bloody Battle of Bloody Marsh was over, with Montiano later reporting just seven Spanish casualties.

The Spanish stayed at Fort St. Simon's for a week, planning another attack. They changed their minds and decided to get out when Oglethorpe leaked false information that British reinforcements were coming from Charlestown. In a snit, they destroyed the fort on their way out.

The Battle of Bloody Marsh is reenacted yearly on St. Simon's Island.

ETOWAH INDIAN MOUNDS • CARTERSVILLE

The Mississippian Culture was the last pre-historic cultural development in North America. They thrived from approximately 800 AD until the arrival of the Europeans.

Today, the Etowah Indian Mounds Historic Site is one of the nation's best examples of life in the Mississippian Culture. Spread across the 54-acre site are six earthen mounds, a plaza, and a village area. Excavations of the site have uncovered spectacular artifacts that depict the everyday life of Mississippians, including shell

Etowah Indian Mounds Historic Site is one of the nation's best examples of the Mississippian Culture.
Photo by Zeny Williams

beads, copper ear ornaments, paints, tattoos, and pottery. These items are on display in the museum.

Events are held throughout the year to educate visitors on

Georgia's Native American heritage. You can learn flintknapping—the art of making arrow heads from stone—basketweaving, pottery making, and weaponry. There are also periodic nighttime tours, where you can tour the mounds by torchlight.

FORT KING GEORGE • DARIEN

Georgia's oldest fort, Fort King George, was built in 1721 by Colonel John "Tuscarora Jack" Barnwell to defend Great Britain's southern colonies from Spanish and French invasion. The fort consisted of a blockhouse, soldiers' barracks, officers' quarters, and a guard house, which also served as a hospital when needed.

Barnwell had requested a group of robust young soldiers for his new fort, but instead he received a company of out-pensioners—veterans retired because of age or injury—who had been called back to duty. The trip over from England was exceedingly hard on these soldiers, and many faced a lengthy hospital recovery in South Carolina before reporting for duty. As a result, the garrison, which was called His Majesty's Independent Company of Foot, did not go into service at Fort George until 1722.

Life was hard for the soldiers at Fort George. Many of them died within the first year to be replaced by irregulars and Swiss Army deserters. Conditions were horrendous, and so many soldiers wanted to leave so badly that in 1724, the fort was burned under mysterious circumstances.

It was rebuilt, this time with substandard materials, making conditions even worse. With desertions commonplace, the

ability of the fort
to mount an
adequate defense
against even the
smallest
aggression was
questionable. In
1727, it was finally
shut down and fell
to disrepair.

The fort has been
reconstructed on its
original site, and

Beyond one of the six-pounder cannons on naval carriages are the
officers' quarters (on the left) and the enlisted men's barracks of
Fort King George.
Photo by Ed Mathews
Copyright 2004 Amelia Island Images

today hosts living history events throughout the year. There are
such events as Oglethorpe at Darien, where the visit of General
Oglethorpe to the young settlement of Darien is recreated;
Scottish Heritage Days, which reenacts the Battle of Bloody
Marsh and honors the Highlanders who fought in that battle;
and Cannons Across The Marsh, an Independence Day
celebration, featuring artillery and musket drills, and the
recreation of life as a Revolutionary soldier.

THE SIEGE OF SAVANNAH • SAVANNAH

The Siege of Savannah was fought on October 9, 1779. The
British had captured Georgia the year before, and the Colonials
wanted it back. Since September, the American Militia and their
French allies had been amassing forces on Tybee Island. On
September 16, French Admiral Count Charles Henri d'Estaing

called upon the British to surrender to his superior forces, making the huge mistake of giving them twenty-four hours to think it over.

During that twenty-four hours, the British used five hundred slaves to vastly improve their defenses, increasing their fortifications from four to thirteen and mounting more than one hundred cannons. On September 17, the answer was firm: "No. Come and get us."

The attack began at 2 a.m. on October 9, with Continental forces attacking at the Spring Hill Redoubt, the weakest of the British defenses. The fighting lasted only an hour before the allies realized it was a futile battle. Retreat was sounded, with more than eight hundred allied forces suffered casualties, including Count Casimir Pulaski, the Polish general who showed immense bravery during the American Revolution and whom Georgia has honored by naming a town and a county for him. The British, who reported only eighteen casualties in the siege, occupied Savannah for three more years.

The battle was the second bloodiest of the American Revolutions, with Bunker Hill having the dubious honor of being the first. An historic marker has been erected at the site of the mass grave where the hundreds killed in the battle are buried. A commemorative ceremony honoring the battle's dead is conducted yearly, and reenactments of the Siege of Savannah are held periodically.

Historical Events Around Georgia

WORMSLOE HISTORIC SITE • SAVANNAH

The Wormsloe Historic Site lies on a breathtaking, oak-lined avenue in historic Savannah. The colonial estate was constructed by Noble Jones, one of Georgia's first settlers.

Jones came to Savannah in 1733 with his friend James Oglethorpe, who charged Jones with much responsibility in the new colony. An English physician and carpenter, Jones commanded a company of Marines charged with Georgia's coastal defense. Oglethorpe appointed him the colony's constable, and he served as an Indian agent and a surveyor, who laid out the fledgling colonies of New Ebenezer and Augusta. When Savannah's physician died, he took over that responsibility as well.

Oglethorpe awarded Jones a lease on five hundred acres on the Isle of Hope, ten miles from Savannah. It was here that he constructed a home on the land he named "Wormslow." He developed the place as a working plantation, adding outbuildings and planting experimental gardens that became a Savannah attraction.

Today, visitors can tour the ruins of Wormsloe and view artifacts excavated from there and a film about the founding of the thirteenth colony. A nature trail leads to the living history area, where during special events, costumed artisans, storytellers, and musicians demonstrate the life and skills of the early colonists. Events are scheduled throughout the year.